PRAISE FOR

"Being and staying visible in the workplace of today is challenging. Susan Barber's new book, *The Visibility Factor*, provides actionable tools and relatable stories so you can be authentically you *and* stay visible in your organization. Infused with compassion, heart and soul, *The Visibility Factor*, is the book you need if you are ready to elevate your leadership and impact within your company."

—Carson Tate, author of *Own It. Love It. Make it Work.*

"Too many times I see leaders playing small due to their own fears. Through her personal experience as well as those clients she has coached, Susan M. Barber provides the reader with a process to identify and go beyond those limiting beliefs. Her stories resonate because they are what we have all experienced in our careers and lives. Even the most adept leaders have had an experience where they stepped back because they didn't think they were enough. Susan's 4-step process can help even the most reticent reader step into their authentic self."

—Lynn P. Sontag, CEO and Owner, Menttium Corporation

"An inspirational guide written by a seasoned leadership coach on how to make a visible impact at a company and be seen for your true talent."

—Kelley Bruemmer, VP of Merchandising and Design, Peepers

"It is often said that we teach what it is we need to learn. Susan Barber has reinvented herself as the foremost leading expert on creating visibility in the workplace. Each chapter of her book is packed with inspirational stories and new ideas for creating more visibility, not only the workplace but your life. As a coach who works with executives, I'll be gifting my clients with this book. It's a must read!"

—Karen Davis, Executive Coach and coauthor of
How to Get the Most Out of Coaching, A Client's Guide for Optimizing the Coaching Experience

"Susan Barber's *The Visibility Factor* creates a welcoming virtual coach experience for each reader to successfully step out of the shadows to build their confidence, showcase their value and go after the career of their dreams! She masterfully shares stories that illustrate why hard work will only take you so far. If you are ready for your authentic value and capabilities to be visible and rewarded, then read this book and discover how to be seen for all that you offer!"

—Mary Tess Rooney, Author of *Heart Value* and Host of True Stride Podcast

"An inspiring read regardless of level in an organization - whether just starting out, looking to take the next step or in a leadership role. Written with honesty, personal experience, research and reflection……..a must read!"

—Peggy Plohg, Director, Organization Effectiveness, Molex

"*The Visibility Factor* helps leaders learn how to be visible, improve visibility to their team, their management, and up the ladder. I wish I had had this book in my reference library from the moment I graduated college as I went into the business world. I had many aha moments as I read the book where I could see the missed opportunities and missteps in my career that this book would have helped me to avoid. A great read and applicable to all levels of leadership!"

—Mona Reiser, Chief Operating Officer, Access Education Holding Corp.

The Visibility Factor

BREAK THROUGH YOUR FEARS,
STAND IN YOUR OWN POWER
AND BECOME THE AUTHENTIC LEADER
YOU WERE MEANT TO BE

SUSAN M. BARBER

The Visibility Factor:
Break Through Your Fears, Stand in Your Own Power and Become the
Authentic Leader You Were Meant to Be

Copyright © 2021 Susan M. Barber.

All rights reserved. No part or any portion of this book may be reproduced in any form, mechanical or digital, or transmitted without the prior written permission of the author, except for the use of brief quotations in a book review.

Some names and identifying details have been changed to protect the privacy of individuals.

This book is presented solely for educational and entertainment purposes. It is the intent of the author to provide general knowledge and helpful information on the subjects discussed to assist readers in their quest for greater understanding and utilization of the ideas, thoughts and principles presented. The advice and strategies contained herein may not be suitable for your situation.

ISBN-13: 978-1-7376104-4-1 (Trade Paperback)
ISBN-13: 978-1-7376104-6-5 (Digital Online)
ISBN-13: 978-1-7376104-2-7 (Audio File)

Library of Congress Control Number: 2021914571

Cover and Book Design by CB Messer
Cover Photography ©depositphotos.com/3dconceptsman
Edited by Zoë Bird
Proofread by KellyAnn Bessa

Printed in the United States of America.

First printing edition 2021
Susan M. Barber
P.O. Box 913
Lake Villa, IL 60046

https://susanmbarber.com

10 9 8 7 6 5 4 3 2 1

To my parents, my angels up in heaven who watch over me and all that I do: I know that the lessons I have learned along the way started with you. I am using my voice just like you encouraged me to do. I hope you are watching from the stands. Miss you both.

Contents

Introduction – 1

Chapter 1:
WHEN THE STUDENT IS READY, THE TEACHER APPEARS – 24

Chapter 2:
FOLLOW YOUR OWN VISIBILITY PATH – 56

Chapter 3:
ASK FOR HELP! – 81

Chapter 4:
THE INVISIBLE CHALLENGE OF VISIBILITY – 104

Chapter 5:
DON'T GIVE IN, RISE UP! – 125

Chapter 6:
THAT'S A GREAT IDEA! – 142

Chapter 7:
THE ULTIMATE BATTLE: IMPOSTOR SYNDROME – 182

Chapter 8:
IT'S DRAFT DAY! – 220

Chapter 9:
WHAT'S THE SCORE? – 240

Chapter 10:
IT'S TIME TO STEP UP! – 252

Chapter 11:
IT'S YOUR TURN TO SHINE! – 272

Appendix – 287

RISE Framework Step One – Reflect:
ADDITIONAL EXAMPLES – 289

Endnotes – 297

Acknowledgments – 303

About the Author – 305

Introduction

ELISE LOOKED AROUND AS SHE closed her manager's door. She was so close to tears, she prayed that no one else was in the hall.

Kim, her manager, had called Elise in to give her feedback before everyone left for the Christmas holiday. Elise was stunned at what she had been told—that the promotion which had been dangled in front of her for months would not happen after all. The feedback had been harsh, and Elise felt as if she couldn't succeed in this role no matter what changes she made. She was blindsided. *Who calls somebody in right before they leave for the Christmas holiday and says all that? Kim is the Grinch, and her heart is definitely three sizes too small! I don't understand her at all. She isn't happy unless everyone else is miserable!* That morning, Elise had been filled with so much excitement when she thought about leaving the next day to see her family. Now she felt like Rudolph did when the other reindeer discovered his red nose—alone and abandoned because he didn't fit in. No one could cheer him up in that moment, and Elise felt the same.

Elise couldn't wait to get out of the building at the end of the day; she probably should have left right after that conversation happened. Her body was in the rest of the day's meetings, but her mind was somewhere else. She couldn't focus on anything but what her boss had said to her, and vacillated from anger at Kim to disappointment in herself. She left the building and blended in among the other commuters as she walked to catch her bus, her mind replaying the conversation from earlier in the day. *How on earth will I deal with this? How will I face her after vacation?*

As she boarded the bus, all the concerns she'd had when she accepted her current, global role two years before flooded back over her. Elise had known it would be a challenge to work for Kim, who was smart and politically astute but had a reputation as a control freak and a micromanager. Prior to their working together, Elise had considered Kim a friend, so she didn't think Kim would act that way toward her. Instead, Elise saw how successful Kim was and couldn't wait to learn from her. She could see how this role would provide the exposure to senior management that she needed and the international perspective that she had always wanted.

However, a few months into the role, Elise realized that Kim's reputation couldn't compare to the reality. It was worse than she could have ever imagined. *How can she be viewed as successful when she manipulates and controls everyone like puppets?* Although Elise tried to build her own visibility, Kim wanted to be the star of the show. She was insecure and uninterested in an understudy who might take her part away. The spotlight had to be on her, or she would find a way to take it. She criticized the people on her team publicly and privately. Elise wasn't allowed to make any decisions, and she had to have Kim's approval on everything she did. Most days, Elise walked on eggshells because she never knew whether the "good Kim" or the "bad

Introduction

Kim" would show up. This environment caused Elise to second-guess all her decisions, and she lost her confidence.

Elise had hoped that the relationship would get easier once there was more trust built between her and Kim, but that trust never materialized. She felt paralyzed, unable to move forward in any way for fear of criticism. This was a dream role for Elise, but could she be successful in it? She looked out the bus window at the shoppers walking through the city under the Christmas lights, their shopping bags full of gifts, and wished that she could go back to that morning and feel the Christmas joy again. She watched raindrops fall down the window and realized that she had started to cry. She could no longer hold in the tears she'd been suppressing all day. She felt as if she had no options, and silently wondered what she should do next.

I had coached Elise for a few years and through a few career transitions. We had a call scheduled the next day, and she started off the call with the recent Kim situation. I could hear how hurt and angry she was, and that her energy was lower than usual. She was happy to leave town for the holidays, but this situation had cast a dark cloud over her mood. She hoped that the time with her family and the familiar scenery of her hometown would give her an energy boost. I asked if she would like to find a time to meet in person while she was home, and could hear the excitement in her voice as she said, "YES!" Her family lives about four hours away from me, so we chose a spot halfway between to meet for lunch and a half-day, deep coaching session.

I have named these sessions "Daring Breakthroughs" because they give clients the space to really slow down, focus, think bigger, and move out of their comfort zones. I love this type of coaching session because a client will walk in with low energy, overwhelmed, but then leave the session filled with energy and motivated to go execute the plan they've just created.

We drove to the local library when we met to see if they had any small rooms that we could use for our session. We found an ideal room that had windows, a long table, and a whiteboard that spanned the length of the room.

We talked about the conversation that she'd had with her boss. It was difficult for Elise to talk about, and brought out a lot of tears. She was still in shock at the blunt way the feedback had been delivered. It made her feel hopeless.

My goal is to always help the client move forward and focus on the positives, so I asked her to share what she had accomplished throughout the year. She talked about what she had done to grow her team, and the big results that they had achieved. We captured each one on the whiteboard so she could see that this one situation with Kim did not take away from all her other accomplishments. I asked her to look at the past year and think about it as if it were a movie. I asked her, "What would you title it?" She answered with a smile, "*Lost My Mojo!*" It was powerful for her to name it. She had dried her tears and her energy began to increase. We drew a metaphorical line in the sand (okay, we had no sand, so I drew a line on the whiteboard... use your imagination!) and I said, "All that has happened is now in the past." It was time to move forward.

I moved the direction of the conversation to focus on the goals Elise wanted to accomplish. It was important she see that this one situation with her boss did not define her. Just because a manager gives an employee feedback doesn't mean

Introduction

that the employee has to accept it without question. However, the employee should try and look at the feedback objectively.

In Elise's case, we asked: Was any of it true? Was her manager right about how she had shown up during the past year? How did she want to be more visible and confident in the new year? The goal was to have her see that the new year could be a blank slate. She could decide who she wanted to be and create a plan to get there.

Our session was an opportunity for Elise to gain new perspective, build her confidence back up, and discuss how she wanted to move forward, toward specific outcomes. At the end of the session, everything about her was different. The tears and frustration had disappeared. She smiled, sat up straighter, and was ready to get started on her plan. I asked her what she would title the movie she wanted to create for the new year. She thought about it for a moment and responded, "*The Year of Wonder Woman!*" We talked about what that meant to her, what she would do differently, and how she would live that way every day. She was so excited that she started work on the follow-ups that same night.

Her plan included new ways to show up differently for herself. She planned to focus on actions that would push her out of her comfort zone and shift her self-perception. The main goal of these actions was to increase her visibility with leaders besides her manager. A few weeks later, she took the bold action of meeting with the president of her company. That initiative paid off when he announced that he would put her in charge of a global program, one of the big bets of the company for the year. She would get a chance to demonstrate her new confidence, change the perceptions that people had of her, and show them the value she could bring to the organization. She bought some cuffed bracelets like Wonder Woman's as a reminder of the leader that she wanted to be.

People Don't Leave Companies, They Leave Managers

Elise's story is an example of how a leader with a strong, overbearing personality can shift how an employee sees themselves and kill their confidence. This causes the person to want to hide, or avoid any hint of criticism that could come their way. Elise had put her manager on a pedestal and trusted that Kim would support her development. Kim had a different agenda. Elise wanted to avoid criticism, so she gave Kim's opinions more weight and importance than her own. She could no longer see that her own thoughts and ideas were valuable. I have many clients who have come to me with similar stories of leaders who want to control and disempower their team members.

Leaders have the power to raise their teams up or bring them down. The leadership of a team has a weight of responsibility that some people handle well, while others struggle to carry it. The old saying goes, "People don't leave companies, they leave managers." A bad manager who creates drama and, in some cases, a hostile work environment is a serious problem. Unfortunately, too many leaders are insecure and make things miserable for everyone who works for them. Such leaders don't leverage the talent of their employees, but criticize or diminish what their team members do instead. The team members are faced with the decision to either find a way to work around the situation or leave.

Introduction

Elise really loved her role and wanted to stay at the company. She chose to ask for help so she could find a way to handle conversations with her boss in a different way and create her own visibility in the company, beyond her boss. If you are in a similar situation with your leadership, you can ask for help, too. Don't hide your value or let someone diminish you.

Coming Out of the Shadow of Invisibility

I COULD SEE SO MUCH of my own story in what happened to Elise. I had been in a similar position and realized that I was stuck, so I made the decision to move out of the background where I had been for so long. That was eleven years ago, when I started to focus on how to be more visible. I thought that it would be a walk in the park for me to change what I did and be seen differently: I would read some books, follow what they said to do and abracadabra... I would be visible! But it wasn't that simple.

I saw other people speak up in meetings and watched what they did to get in front of their management. I could have done the exact same things, but that wouldn't have been me. I would have felt as if I were being political and boastful, which was inauthentic and felt false to me. I had to figure out how to overcome my fear and stand out in my own, authentic way.

It took me a while to reflect and look at the stories I told myself. I needed to decide if these stories supported me anymore and determine what actions to take to stop being "invisible." What I found through this self-discovery was not what I expected. I had to accept the fact that I had unconsciously chosen invisibility. I had chosen to sit in the back of the room because of my belief that higher-level people should sit at the table. I had chosen not to speak up because I thought other people's opinions were more important than my own.

You may ask yourself, *Why on earth would she choose to do that?* I had to spend some time to work through that and find the answers. I realized that I had chosen to play small and not use my voice because it was the safer option. It allowed me to avoid failure and stay out of the politics that are amplified at senior levels in an organization. I could handle a senior leadership role now, but back then I wasn't prepared. Have you been through something similar in your career? Have you worked hard, but can't seem to move ahead? Have you made a choice to be invisible? If you answered yes, then you are in the right place, my friend.

Although this book was written with corporate leaders in larger companies in mind, the principles can apply to leaders at any level in any size company. For example, a senior leader could share the book with a team member who needs help with visibility, a leader who was recently promoted or a recent college graduate who is about to enter the workforce in a corporate role. What is included here can be adapted to your situation.

On the other side of this visibility journey you are about to take is a much better place, a place that allows you to be yourself. Not the person that someone else wants you to be; just you, exactly as you are.

I wore a mask of invisibility for so many years, and had no idea that I'd done that to myself. No one else told me to be a certain way. I compared myself to other people and made assumptions about what I should do. I worked so hard and delivered what was asked of me, but I couldn't move forward. I assumed that if I could be what leadership wanted, and acted

Introduction

in a certain way, then I would be accepted and get a promotion. I tried to fit in and be the person that my management wanted me to be. It wasn't their fault; I made those choices to try and win the promotion prize. It caused me so much internal conflict and drained my energy every day.

Does this happen for you, too? Do you feel as if you have to be someone else at work? Let me share another option with you. Stop the self-judgment and comparison with others. You get to make a different choice that is focused on you and what you want. This is an opportunity to make choices that work with your style, show others your value and help you see the career possibilities that exist for you!

The transformational journey that I have been on to learn about myself and figure out who I am is the best thing that I could have done. I don't say that lightly. When I started, I was deeply skeptical that I could change. But I was also tired of a life focused on fear, perfection and a lack of confidence. It wasn't helpful to me, and it made me feel worse about myself. I compared myself to others and knew I had to try a different approach to get past it. I had to figure out a new path for myself, regain my confidence and find a way to get my energy back.

Now it is your turn to focus on you. You have a guide right here to help you take this journey. You will not be alone; I will be with you every step of the way.

You are worth it. Trust me.

Visibility and Its Value

THE QUESTION IS, DO YOU believe that you are worth it? You may not, yet, and that is okay. You may still have some skepticism about your self-worth because you put everyone else first. I used to feel that way, too. And I was ashamed that I had not seen the signs and asked for help sooner. I don't want anyone else to feel that shame. I created *The Visibility Factor* to help show people that they can shift how they see themselves, and how others see them, if they put some intention and focus into their actions. Many people believe that all they have to do is work hard, that if they show up and get the work done, that is all that is necessary to be seen. In the next few chapters, however, you will learn that more than hard work is required to gain visibility.

Before we go there, though, let's look at some examples of how you may see yourself. These beliefs and thoughts could affect how you act if you aren't as visible as your management wants you to be:

- You are told that you need to be visible, but don't know what actions to take to be seen.
- You see others get the promotions or leadership roles you want, but don't know what to do to get the same things for yourself.
- You continue to do what you always have done. This helped you get to where you are, but as you climb higher, you find it doesn't work anymore.
- Deep down inside, you have a sense that you need to do more, but that is too scary to think about because you might fail. You can't lose your reputation, so you engage in self-sabotage, blame others, and stay busy behind the scenes in the hopes that someone will notice you.

Introduction

- You rationalize that your performance is enough to get you promoted. You don't have time to do this extra stuff to get in front of people and show them what you can do. Your work should speak for itself without you having to "play politics."
- You work hard and deliver on what you committed to do. You may be an overachiever and competitive, but it still isn't enough to get to the next level.
- You have had success in your career, but your fear and limiting beliefs hold you back from greater success. You stay safe this way and avoid failure.
- You don't want to compromise who you are to become more visible, so you don't do anything different.
- You want to climb the ladder and enjoy the success that you know in your heart you can achieve, and get frustrated when it doesn't happen.
- You are intimidated by the chain of command and titles. You tend to put people on a pedestal and give your power away to others. You are reactive instead of proactive and have low confidence.
- You hide behind a fear of judgment and criticism, and behind the stronger voices in the room. You compare your own accomplishments with theirs. Although other people believe in you, you don't believe in yourself and sabotage opportunities.

This is quite a list. Each one of these examples came from clients and coworkers of mine who have held these beliefs or been given these messages. When they talk about how they feel inside, they avoid eye contact as their shame and disappointment take over, diminishing their energy and increasing their stress level. It is less about what their managers say to them and more about the larger impact on their self-image, which lasts far beyond a conversation. It impacts how the person who received the feedback sees themselves and gets in the way of the work that they try to do each day. The weight of this feedback sits on their shoulders and it feels hopeless. They are frustrated and can't see a way to fix it. To use a baseball metaphor, they take themselves out of the game or give up before they step up to the plate to take a swing at the ball. They accept their fate because they can't see a way to change their situation. If you can see yourself in any of the above examples, please know that, no matter what obstacle shows up, there is always a choice. I promise you it is not hopeless. You will learn how to move past it.

The long list above is how I used to see myself, too. Somewhere along the way, in my career, I lost my confidence and belief in myself. I sought out external validation from others to tell me that I did a good job, but I tended not to believe people when they said I did well. That is how deep these stories and beliefs were buried. I made the choice to find a way to change for myself. You can make that choice too.

The dreams of my ideal career started back when I was a little girl. My sister and I would go to my mom's office sometimes and play pretend work! I watched my mom climb the ladder at her company and I longed to do the same. She started at General Foods as a secretary after high school and progressed until she became the only woman among the senior staff at her location. It appeared to be such a great job to me, and I wanted a similar role. I wanted to emulate her when I grew up. I imagined the limo that would pick me up to go to the airport for a business trip, a closet full of business suits and an office of my own, the same as Mom had.

I achieved that dream and was lucky enough to create a bigger one. During my twenty-five-plus years at Kraft Heinz (and Kraft's many iterations throughout those years), I leveraged the strong work ethic that my parents taught me, and it helped me climb the ladder even higher than I'd envisioned. (Not long after I started working at Kraft, Philip Morris, the company that owned General Foods, acquired us. For a short time before my mom retired, we worked for the same company!) I traveled the globe and led teams locally and globally, and my teams implemented projects and systems that everyone said were impossible to deliver. I was the person who was called in when there was big problem to solve or a team to turn around. I built strong relationships with people, created trust quickly and had a reputation for my ability to lead a team and get a lot of work done.

Impostor Syndrome

I WAS WELL-RESPECTED AND CREDIBLE in the organization, and I focused every day on ensuring that I set a great example as a leader. I knew deep down that if I worked hard, I could be a senior leader in the future. But at a certain level in a company, hard work is not enough, and I unconsciously hid behind other people and found ways to sabotage my own future opportunities. Every time I tried to do more, fear would show up and I would rationalize why someone else should take the responsibility. I couldn't reconcile how everyone else saw me versus how I saw myself. Doubts, fear, and a lack of confidence swirled around in my head. No matter how much I did, I never thought I was good enough. I had impostor syndrome in a bad way, but I didn't know it.

People with impostor syndrome are overachievers who feel as if they don't know enough and live in fear that everyone will eventually find out. The external view of people with impostor syndrome is that they are high performers. Internally, though, people with impostor syndrome see themselves as never good enough and unable to compete with everyone else.

I lived with a complete lack of confidence and played small. The fear of failure was a constant and became the lens through which I viewed everything, both personally and professionally. (You will learn more about impostor syndrome in Chapter 4.)

My Next Career Chapter

IN 2015, I MADE THE difficult choice to leave Kraft Heinz when the company went through a merger. I could have stayed, but I knew in my gut that it was time for me to go on to part two of my career. The choice to leave was scary because my identity was inextricably tied to Kraft; I had been with the company almost as long as I had been married. All my friends worked there, and it was my foundation and security. I taught at a nearby university and attended an online coach school at night with a plan to become a coach "someday," far into the future. With this new situation, I had to accelerate my "someday" plan to a "right now" plan. I was excited about the new possibilities. I would have to learn how to stand on my own; I would no longer have the Kraft name and credibility attached to my own.

Introduction

I believe that things happen for a reason in your life, although you can't always see why at the time. Two weeks before I was supposed to leave the company, I had to fly to Dallas for a sales meeting. I told my dad that my last day with the company would be August 15. As I sat on the plane and waited for takeoff, he sent me a Facebook message that said, "Be safe, and keep your chin up! You are tough like your mother, you will get through this!!! Love ya, Dad." He hardly ever said stuff like that, and it brought me to tears. My mom had passed away from cancer fifteen years before and it had been hard without her. She was always the one I would have talked to in these big life situations. My dad had watched my mom leave the company when she retired, so he knew that this transition would be a big deal for me, though I didn't know it myself yet.

After my last day at the company, Dad mentioned that he hadn't felt that great. My entire family called him "hard as nails" because he was always the tough guy who got through stuff on his own and avoided doctors whenever possible. I went to the doctor with him, and it was worse than we thought. It was stage four cancer, and it had spread to multiple places. Having watched what my mom went through, he chose not to do any treatment. He wanted to be at home.

Five weeks from the day I left my job, with my sister and me by his side, he went to join my mom in heaven. I thought about it afterwards and realized: This was the reason that I needed to leave my job. It gave me the gift of time to spend with my dad in the last month he was with us. I am so grateful that I made the decision I did.

The next five months were focused on executing his estate and the sale of his house. I had lots of time to think—maybe too much. I had been this big career woman, and suddenly I didn't have that identity anymore. I felt a little lost, to be honest. It was so bizarre to have no meetings to attend, no conference calls to join. I knew I had to make some decisions about what I would do next, and I had two options in mind: I could go back into a corporate role or start my own coaching business. The latter was the scarier choice because I had never had my own business before. Someone once told me that the choice that scares you the most is the one you are supposed to pick. I made the decision that I would start my own business, focused on leadership development coaching and consulting.

The Birth of the Visibility Factor

IN FEBRUARY OF 2016, I completed the paperwork to start my own business. I wanted people to see me as a leadership coach and thought leader, not an IT person from Kraft. I had to do something different than I had ever done to make that shift. As my first attempt to establish credibility in my new role, I began to write a blog. I blogged every weekday for eighteen months. Some of my former colleagues read the blogs and reached out to begin working with me as their coach. As I started to work with corporate clients, I was surprised to see how much more I had learned at Kraft than I realized. We had been given so many business and leadership experiences that set us up for success no matter where we worked. Not all companies offered that to their teams. Some of those experiences were hard, but I was grateful for what I learned about leadership, how to build a team and how to be visible. What I learned from my own career experiences was what helped me to step out of the shadows

Introduction

and into the spotlight in this new business. I could do so much with my business, but deep down inside me was another dream, one that I had never talked about with anyone.

When I was about two years old, my mom signed me up for my first library card at the public library. I loved to go to the library and pick out a stack of books. When I was older, you could find me inside a Borders bookstore for hours on a Sunday afternoon (I was so sad when it went out of business). Books were always the first place I looked when I wanted to learn more about a topic or needed some inspiration. I wondered: Could I write a book that would help leaders see that they could be visible in ways authentic to them? The book that I couldn't find but wanted for myself when I needed it many years ago? My dream was to help leaders that were feeling invisible like me and write that book.

Once I started to share my book dream with other people, they encouraged me to write it. I began to believe it was possible. *The Visibility Factor* book idea was born, and it became a goal for me to write it. I joined a workshop that would help me write a book, but it gave me so much more than I expected. I found a supportive community of other would-be authors who became my friends as we went on the journey together.

Create Your Authentic Visibility

TWO WOMEN IN MY BOOK workshop asked me to read their books and give them feedback. When I read their books, I was in shock! Our stories were very different, but we'd all had similar experiences. We came from different parts of the United States and had different types of careers, and yet we all had the same issues. We lived with self-doubt and low self-worth, and went through situations that damaged our confidence and held us back. We are only three people who happened to meet in a book group, and we have all been through the same challenges.

It made me wonder: How many other people in the world are impacted by these same kinds of issues? How could I do something bigger to help others so fewer people have to live in doubt or fear? It pains me to think of people who suffer with this struggle every day. *The Visibility Factor* was created to show leaders how to raise their visibility and give them back the confidence that they lost along the way.

I use a process that I created to help people create their visibility plan. I usually use it in one-on-one conversation, but I wanted to test it with a group. I built a course called "Create Your Authentic Visibility" to test the process so I could make changes if needed to include in the book. Each participant in the group had their own story of why they weren't in front of their management more often, why it wasn't a priority or they avoided it all together. At the start of the course, I asked some of the participants what prevented them from taking actions that increase their visibility. Here are a few of their answers:

- "I worry about being visible in a not-so-great way. If you make a mistake—especially if it's one that costs the company money—you have made yourself visible in the opposite direction."
- "I tend to take on multiple tasks without delegating or sharing all the work I have done with my manager, just because I feel some things are not important enough to share or it feels as if I am bragging."

Introduction

- "I have fear that I do not know all the answers. I also have a fear of reprisal if I happen to say something that is not… acceptable or appropriate."

The responses were from a small sample of attendees, but they mirror what I have heard from so many people; there's a common theme of fear. Hearing these responses brought back the same feelings I had when I was told I wasn't visible enough. I once operated from that same place of fear and didn't trust myself enough. I needed to learn all these lessons the hard way, but I don't want that to be your journey.

I believe in meeting people wherever they are when we talk about what they want in their careers. When visibility is one of their challenges, they usually fall into one of these three categories:

- **Getting Started**—Have minimal experience with and focus on visibility.
- **Some Experience**—Have tried to do some things to stand out, but want to do more and improve skills.
- **Experienced**—Have visibility, but want to do more to expand higher-level influence.

Whatever category you feel you fit into is fine. There is no right or wrong place to be. You will be able to use the process that I created in the book to help you build a visibility plan. It will help you understand where you are, look at what you want to accomplish, and build a plan from the easy-to-follow steps to get you there.

A Proven Process

I HAVE SEEN ALL MY clients and class participants try the visibility ideas and experience a shift. Their confidence grows and they are motivated to do more. Throughout this book, you will read many stories of people who have used this process and can now see themselves the way that everyone else sees them. I love to hear their stories and I am honored to be able to help them. I want to help you to rise up out of the background and be the star that shines with confidence.

Are you still a bit skeptical? It's okay. Unless you know me IRL (in real life), why should you trust that I can help you? What sets me apart from anyone else who says they coach people on leadership and visibility? Do you wonder if you can do what the people in the book have done? All I ask is for you to extend me the benefit of the doubt for these reasons: I have been where you are and on this same journey to become visible. As long as they work their plan, every person I have ever coached to use this process has increased their confidence, found new ways to show their value, and shifted their perception after its completion. And I haven't seen another book that provides a one-stop shop for increasing visibility via an easy-to-follow process with a coach alongside you as your guide. The resources and real client examples are here for you to see what others have done with their plans so you can learn from their experiences. In this book, I will share all the insights, resources, and tools that helped me work through my own challenges with visibility. I will also share some stories of other leaders who have had this same issue. (All names that are used in these stories have been changed to protect coworkers' and clients' privacy.)

Introduction

I became a coach to help business leaders shine a light on their leadership, create the career they were meant to have, and illuminate the path for those whom they lead. My role as coach is to help people accelerate their performance, show their value, and increase their confidence so they can move up to the next level. Let me be your virtual coach and help you, too. My goal is for you to learn from my mistakes and those of others who have shared their stories here. There is no need for you to struggle with this on your own. Take our lessons and apply them for yourself. Ask for support to help you integrate these lessons faster. Use this book as a tool to help you find your own visibility strategy and begin to execute it today. You have unique gifts that people need to see, and hiding them from yourself and other people doesn't help you. You need to step out in front of people and let them see who you are and what you can do.

In my years as a coach, I have been witness to so many leaders overcoming their fear and increasing their confidence. Everyone deserves that moment when they realize they have shifted their perception of themselves and no longer need or want to hide behind anyone else. Everyone can be authentic in their own leadership, use their voice and show their value.

An Extraordinary Time for Leaders

BEFORE YOU MOVE ON TO Chapter 1, I would be remiss not to mention the outbreak of COVID-19 that caused a seismic shift in everyone's lives in 2020. This book was in process at this time of uncertainty for the whole world. Everyone felt the impact of the virus in such profound ways, and it seems as if it will continue to be felt for many years to come. Mental health struggles are not something that many leaders had to think about with their teams in the past—however, they are no longer an optional part of the conversation. Leaders have to be compassionate as employees deal with loss and anxiety while trying to focus on their work.

No one knows what the ongoing work environment will look like as we move to the post-pandemic world, but I am a strong believer that change brings opportunities. My hope is that you can leverage the ideas that are shared in the book to help you successfully navigate the changes that occur. In Chapter 10, I include some information on how people can gain visibility for themselves and their teams while working in a remote environment. For some, this will become the new normal, and I share ideas for how to remain in front of your management when you aren't physically there.

Here Are a Few Last Tips

I BUILT IN AN AREA for notes at the end of each chapter. If you need more space, you may want to grab a shiny new notebook or find some paper and your favorite pen to capture your extra notes. (You can choose to type them to capture notes electronically too, but it has been proven that writing things down helps you retain them longer.)[1]

You will find action steps at the end of each chapter that will help you reinforce the information you read in that chapter. These additional actions should be done at the completion of the chapter prior to beginning the next one. Think of it as an

Introduction

opportunity to process what you learned; this is a marathon, not a sprint. Give yourself the gift of time to think.

Once you reach Chapter 5, you will take the first step in learning the process of creating your own visibility action plan. There are four easy steps to go through and all the resources you need to design a plan that is customized for you!

Okay, are you ready to go? It's time for you to learn the art of visibility! Let's go make this happen!

Chapter 1:
WHEN THE STUDENT IS READY, THE TEACHER APPEARS

"Sue, why are you playing small?"

I was stunned to hear these words from my mentor, Kathy. I felt shame wash over me as I looked at her from across the conference room table and suddenly, everything went into slow motion. I could feel my face grow hot as it turned red with embarrassment. I am one of those lucky Irish girls with fair skin, which meant that whenever I felt the spotlight shine on me, my neck and face turned a bright crimson. Unfortunately, it was one of those things I couldn't control or hide, so I had to learn to accept it.

I was in a one-on-one meeting with Kathy to connect with her and share the latest updates on our different areas of responsibility. I had worked with her for many years, but she had climbed the ladder faster. She was confident, all business, and known for her extreme directness. Just moments before, the meeting had started in such a positive way as we shared updates about our families; but it was clear now that chitchat time was over, and the conversation was quickly escalating into an unexpected feedback session. It was a conversation that I would never forget.

The walls in the small conference room began to close in on me as she said, "You have so much potential, but you sit at the back of the room in meetings and don't say a word. Why do you even show up?" *That was harsh!* "If you don't participate, then you won't add any value. You know that we expect you to step up at this level and set an example for the organization. We can't consider you for your next role until you figure out how to be more visible."

I am sure she said more than that, but I shut down. I was experiencing an example of that moment when the brain's amygdala senses danger and goes into fight, flight, or freeze mode. I weighed my options. If I pushed back too hard and defended myself, it probably wouldn't help. I couldn't begin to move my legs, so flight wasn't a possibility either. Freeze became the only option as my brain struggled to process what Kathy had said.

The words she had spoken were the last I'd ever expected to hear. I felt defensiveness and emotion rise within me, and suddenly felt the pain in my stomach that I get whenever conflict arises. I could feel my eyes start to fill up with tears and did everything in my power to hold them back. *I will not cry in front of her.*

I had always thought of Kathy as someone who was in my corner. She had supported me through many career changes. She was also one of the most influential people in the leadership team, and she could help or hurt my career. After I heard her feedback, I felt as if I had been hit by a truck.

Chapter 1

Just stay calm, whatever you do. Don't say something you will regret. I tried to think of a brilliant response to say in my defense. What I said came out all wrong, though, and I realized it would be better if I just stayed quiet. I was ashamed and embarrassed. All I wanted to do was get the hell out of there. I felt like an animal trapped in a cage with no way to escape. *Is she right? How did I miss this? They told me I was a top talent and that I was in line for a promotion. Obviously, that's not up for discussion now.* My mind raced through all the possible effects this news could have on my career. It was sinking in quickly for me that the foundation I stood on, and thought was so solid, had shifted. Through sheer will, I found a way to hold it together long enough to say thank you for the feedback. Then I left the meeting to figure out what to do next.

I knew that there were other people in my organization who received feedback that they needed to be "more visible." That wasn't me, though. That was the feedback senior management gave to those "other" people. *I am a top talent! They chose me to be in the leadership program. How did the rules change so much, and I had no idea?* I'd assumed that I was doing what I should, since I hadn't received this type of feedback before. Everyone always complimented me on how much I had accomplished. Clearly, though, the hard work wasn't enough this time. The only thing I could think was, *Does she want me to be one of these people who talk incessantly in meetings and brag all the time? Those are the people that we all roll our eyes at when they begin to talk. I don't want to be one of those people. That isn't my style at all.*

As it all started to sink in, I knew I had to look at the feedback more objectively. I knew that when I got defensive, there was a reason. In this case, it was because deep down, I had to admit that she was right—but I didn't want to be called out for it. I had thought I was visible, but it wasn't enough. I had trusted that I was a top talent and become complacent. I had never faced failure in my career before, and Kathy's comments devastated me. I wanted to hide, which was, ironically, the opposite of what I needed to do. *How on earth will I face everyone at work again?*

I don't remember the drive home, but when I got there, I went straight to my bedroom and sat on the edge of the bed. My husband was sitting in a chair nearby as he played a video game on the TV.

He looked at me and said, "What's wrong?" I lay back on the bed and shared all the feedback I had received earlier that day. He sat quietly while I let it all out. Then I finally said what I had thought about all the way home but had been afraid to say out loud before.

I began slowly. "I don't know if I can stay at the company. The feedback I got today means that I need to do some major damage control to change how I'm perceived. I don't know if it's possible to fix, and I don't know where to begin. I may have to leave the company."

My entire identity was tied to Kraft Foods. I had been there about twenty-three years, and always imagined that I would retire from the company. At the time I started to work, after college, it was still what everyone did: worked at one place for their whole career and then retired. That was the plan I was supposed to follow. Now what? I had put my heart and soul into my work. I had sacrificed sleep and my family more times than I could count to get the job done. The company had been a part of my entire life. I couldn't imagine not being there. Both my grandpa and my mom had worked at the company

Chapter 1

more than twenty-five-plus years before they retired. I felt this unexpected family responsibility to be there to uphold their legacy with the company. Although they were no longer here to witness it, I still didn't want to disappoint them.

My brain was in a fog and I couldn't think straight. This wasn't the best time to make a life-changing decision about whether to stay or leave. I knew that I needed to take some time to process what I had heard and figure out a plan.

My husband left our bedroom and went out into the kitchen. I lay there for a few minutes more to pull myself together. I didn't want the kids to see their mother fall apart.

I found out later that my husband was worried about me. He reached out to one of my good friends from work and said, "I have never seen her this way before. I am not sure what to do or say." It was true. He had never known a time when I didn't have all the answers or wasn't in control. I had always created the appearance that things were great, but that time had passed. No matter how much I tried to hold it all together, I couldn't do it. The small cracks in the dam had grown larger and I had given up the fight to keep the dam from breaking. The water began to spill out. My energy was gone, and it was time to admit that I just couldn't be what everyone wanted me to be anymore. It was time to retire the crown of perfection that I wore every single day. I needed to figure out who I was and learn what "being visible" meant for me.

Brené Brown Enters My Life

CAN YOU KEEP A SECRET? I will admit to you that I am a bit of a fangirl when it comes to Brené Brown. No, I haven't met her yet, but "meet Brené" is on my bucket list! I love her work on vulnerability and shame. She makes the research she does in these areas accessible for people. If you haven't heard of her, she is a Houston, Texas girl, researcher, author, and speaker. In 2013, she collaborated with Oprah to create a virtual class based on her book *The Gifts of Imperfection*,[2] the first book of hers I read.

Millions of people from all over the world joined her class on Oprah's website. It included videos from Brené, instructions to create an art journal, and interactive discussions. One of the most impactful activities she had us do in that class was take a stand against our attempts at perfectionism (remember my crown?). She gave us the permission to accept ourselves wherever we were in that moment. We could continue to improve in certain areas if we wanted to, but we didn't *need* to. There was no reason to see ourselves as not good enough anymore.

As I looked at the thousands of people who were in the virtual class with me, I realized that they struggled with the same issues I did. It wasn't just me. Brené had given all of us a way to have a conversation with ourselves and others that would help us see that we were worthy. The message was clear: It was time to stop the thoughts that we aren't enough, but instead focus on how we could be greater than we ever imagined. I had struggled to see myself as artistic since I was a child, so I was impressed when I looked at my art journal at the end of class. My creativity had come out of the shadows, where it had been hidden away all my life. Sometimes we need to try to get out of our comfort zone to show others a different side of our capabilities, but it also helps us see ourselves in a new way. Can you think of anything that you have kept hidden for years? Is it time to see if you can bring it out of the shadows?

Avoid Criticism

I LEARNED FROM BRENÉ BROWN that perfectionists do whatever they can to avoid criticism. Before I learned that fact, I thought that perfectionism was a good thing. If you have this trait too, you know the amount of energy it takes to maintain perfection. It is an enormous weight to bear, and you can never let your guard down.

I avoided criticism, but in the case of my conversation at the start of this chapter, I knew that Kathy was right. That whole experience was pivotal for me. I am a big believer in signs that give you direction if you pay attention to them; this sign from Kathy blinked in bright orange neon, so I wouldn't miss it! It was the sign that I needed at that time in my career. I think I knew deep down that I had more potential, but to hear that I didn't take advantage of it was painful. It was a bittersweet gift that gave me the push I needed to make some changes. Although Kathy didn't have to, I am so grateful that she had the guts to tell me the truth. It set me on a new path that got me through that situation, and it gave me the motivation to help others who might struggle too.

How Did I Get into This Position?

AS I EXPLORED ALL THE possible reasons behind my actions, it always came back to fear. The fear of failure was big for me, and I did not want the spotlight shone upon me if I messed up. I didn't want to tarnish the "Sweet Perfect Sue" image I had created and lived by my whole life.

I was the firstborn, and felt since I was a child that I had to maintain that perfect image. Back then, it was a different time, and girls were supposed to follow the rules, be agreeable and keep quiet. Some of the comments from relatives and friends of my parents were, "Susan is always such a good girl," and "We just love having her visit, she is so responsible." I used to watch over my younger sister and cousins when our families got together. It was my first opportunity to try out some basic leadership skills that I would depend on and develop more of later in life. I fit into the role of the perfect, responsible daughter and it made my family proud.

So, I started this perfection habit as a child. Did you notice that I called it a habit? That is what it is. It is a habit that can be stopped or changed with focus and intention. You may seek out perfection now, but you don't to have to if you decide you want to change.

I carried the Sweet Perfect Sue image through all my years of school. I did what was expected to receive praise from the teachers. If you are a perfectionist, this might sound familiar to you. A great example of this occurred when I was in fourth grade. I attended a Catholic grade school, and my teacher that year was Sister Loretta. She was about five feet tall, with short dark hair and glasses. She didn't wear a traditional habit, only the black veil with a black dress and a short black jacket, and looked much older than I believe she was. Sister Loretta was a strict teacher who didn't smile much and was always serious. She didn't seem to have much patience and dealt harshly with

Chapter 1

students who broke her rules. I didn't want any part of that, so I followed the rules to stay on her good side.

Our school, St. Martin's Catholic grade school, had eight classrooms on the main floor and was connected to our church. We didn't change rooms for different classes until fifth grade, so we were in that same fourth grade classroom all day long except for recess. Its windows overlooked the area behind the school. Our desks were turned away from those windows in rows that faced the blackboard so we wouldn't be distracted. My desk was at the end of the row closest to the bookshelves, which held encyclopedias, a dictionary, a globe and, close to where I sat, a black, cast iron bank similar to an old-time cash register. The bank was very heavy if you tried to lift it. It had slots for the different coin sizes and a metal lever that you pulled down to push the coins into the bank. On top was a little display window that showed the total amount of money inside. Sister Loretta encouraged us to bring in coins and put them in the bank for charities and those who were less fortunate. It fascinated me to watch when money was inserted and the lever was pulled. (Maybe this prepared me for future slot machine activity in Las Vegas someday, I can't be sure.)

I loved to put coins in that black bank every day just to watch it work. This daily donation activity was soon noticed by Sister Loretta. She praised me in front of the whole class as an example of how to put others before oneself. Her public praise only reinforced my behavior; from that point on, I felt an obligation to put money into that bank every single day. It also solidified my perception that, in her mind, I was a good girl. Little did I know that she had also planted the seed in me that other people's needs were more important than my own.

I brought my "good girl manual" from school into the workplace and continued to be Sweet Perfect Sue as an adult. The voice in my head said, *It has always worked, so why change?* Perfectionism had become an ingrained habit. One of the rules in the "good girl manual" is that you must be liked and praised. The best way to do that is to agree with people. You don't want to have any conflict or drama, so you bury how you really feel deep down inside. That was the way I operated for so many years. It accomplished the goal that I thought I wanted to attain: I was liked and praised, and avoided any criticism from others. The fear of a call-out in public was huge for me. I lived with a lot of fear, so I walked a tightrope between my comfort zone and any unnecessary attention.

My Belief about Hard Work

I WAS RAISED TO BELIEVE that if you work hard and follow the rules, it will pay off. That belief was so strong for me that I made any sacrifice necessary to get the job done. I'm not proud of this at all, but I was a workaholic; in many situations, work would win if there was choice to be made between it and time with my family and friends. It sucks to say that, but it is the truth. I identified with my job and, to be honest, it made me feel important in front of others. It fed my ego to the point that it took over my common sense at times. People seemed impressed by my extensive travel for business trips and the projects that I worked on. Recognition and praise from other people fed my ego, and I craved that more than I want to admit. I lived with a steady monologue in my head that said I wasn't good enough, so these compliments made me feel better. It was a roller coaster of highs and lows that I dealt with every day.

I had a great team of people who could have done more of the work if I let them, but I felt this huge weight of responsibility on my shoulders. I had to control the situation and make sure I was available should I have to step in. My job required a lot of hours, and there was always some work phone call I needed to be on when instead I could have said no and chosen my family. Being on those calls, though, made me feel important and needed. Nonstop work was part of the ethic that had been instilled in me, and I thought I would someday be rewarded for it with a promotion. I tried to be Superwoman to save the day for the team and myself, but I couldn't see that this approach wasn't good for any part of my life.

My hard work had been recognized and rewarded many times before with promotions that eventually put me at a higher level than I had ever dreamed of. However, each time I reached a new level, my competitive side would show up and I wanted to go to the next one.

Fear of Failure

THE FEEDBACK SESSION WITH KATHY was a pivotal moment. It was the catalyst that led me to start this journey toward finding the meaning of visibility and how to improve it. Back then I wasn't sure where to start, so I knew that it was time to ask for help. I talked to mentors and peers for advice, and they shared some of the bold moves they had taken in their own careers.

When the Student is Ready, the Teacher Appears

I met with people I trusted to give me guidance because, in my eyes, I was a failure. I felt as if I was the only one who had this issue and that everyone else knew what to do. I hoped my mentors would tell me that my situation wasn't that bad and there was some easy way I could fix the predicament I was in. They told me that it would take a lot of work on my part to change, and for people to shift their perception of me. Their advice was both honest and consistent.

My first steps involved finding opportunities to speak up, sit at the table with senior leaders, and spend time with influencers in the organization. I felt a bit nauseated as I thought about these new approaches—my physical reaction to fear. I knew how to get stuff done behind the scenes, but I wasn't sure how to be out in front of people and speak up. What if I said or did the wrong things? This thought brought up my fear of failure in a huge way. I would have to take risks to show up differently, but the work to get past the fear in my head was the bigger battle for me. I knew that the advice I'd received was right; it was up to me to figure out how to take it.

My confidence was shaken and, if I wanted to progress in my career, I had to get it back. As I write this, I can remember how it felt in that moment that I lost my confidence. Anyone who worked with me will be surprised to read how I felt at that time. The girl with the crown of perfection never wanted to show that she didn't have it all together. I hid everything from everyone and kept the brave face on so no one would know that I was a mess inside. Although I had advice from mentors to try, I was still so discombobulated. My thoughts were all over the place. *Can I recover from this? What if I try these recommendations and I fail?*

Chapter 1

Am I the Only One?

I SHARE MY STORY WITH you so you know that playing small can happen to anyone, and that you are not alone if you have felt that it was safer for you to stay in the background although you wanted to play bigger in your career. I bet that, just like me, you work hard every day, try to do it all, and assume your manager knows what you do. Let me be the one to tell you the truth. Your manager has a ton to do and doesn't know what you accomplish from day to day. The rest of the organization may not be aware of what you do either. Have you felt that you must work harder, and then they will notice you? I lived with that mantra for so long. I put on the brave face and kept it all inside. That is a lonely place to be. I felt embarrassment, shame, and frustration—stuck, with no way out.

If you see yourself in any of my stories, you know that you need to try a new path. Let me help you become your own best advocate. You have to find ways to share what you do in a way that works for you. As an executive coach, I help people with this every day now. And though years ago I thought I was the only one who had this fear of speaking up for myself to show the value I bring, the people I work with experience the same challenges. When I write about my experiences in my blog or speak at events, I attract clients with similar struggles.

Here are a few examples of the challenges that hold leaders back from bigger opportunities:

- They work hard, but don't stand out and are not talked about for promotions. They are stuck and can't figure out what they need to do to move up.

- They do what they are asked to do, but then receive feedback that what they do isn't enough, and they need to take additional steps to be noticed. They don't know how to address the challenge of how they are perceived.
- They are in a new role as a manager, and aren't sure how to manage a team. They don't know how to lead people, lead themselves, or manage up to gain visibility for their team. (This is the toughest transition a leader can make.)
- They receive a promotion, but don't shift their approach; they continue to do what they have always done. This transition from one level to the next requires that they show their leadership in a bigger way than before, but they don't know how to do it or choose to avoid it.
- They move to a new company, but struggle to establish themselves and build credibility fast enough. (A new employee has about ninety to one hundred days to demonstrate leadership and capability, and to show the company that they made the right decision in hiring them.)
- They may get feedback that sounds similar to this: "You are doing great. You just need to work on these two to three actions and then you will be ready for the next level." This happens repeatedly so they doubt themselves and feel as if they will never be good enough to get a promotion.

I have taken my clients through my visibility process that I call RISE to address these challenges with great success. You will read some of their stories in this book. Know that you will not go through this alone. I will be with you every step of the way. This book will give you easy-to-follow steps that will help you stand out in the way that works best for you and build the confidence that you thought you couldn't get back.

What Is Visibility?

LET'S STEP BACK FOR A moment and talk about how visibility is defined. *Merriam-Webster* defines visibility as "the quality or state of being visible."[3] You become visible when you stand out from the crowd, when you say or do something that puts the spotlight on you. Does the spotlight seem too scary and uncomfortable to consider? If it does, then you may make the decision to stay in the background. Fear is strong. It can overpower you and keep you behind the scenes. You may not realize on a conscious level that you chose to stay out of the limelight, but your actions have showed others that you do not wish to be seen.

Believe me, I had the exact same fear. Anytime I put myself out there in front of people, it was uncomfortable for me. I lacked confidence, so I didn't think that I could be the visible leader my management wanted me to be. However, as I learned more about fear, I understood that what I felt was my brain's attempt to keep me safe. Did you know that your brain can't tell the difference between real danger and a nonthreatening situation that creates anxiety and fear? It is the same fight, flight, or freeze response that showed up for me earlier in this chapter. The critic in our head says a lot of negative things to keep us safe, and sometimes it is not very kind. It makes us feel bad about ourselves and keeps us from taking action, limiting our growth and development. If you believe its messages, you won't do anything. You will stay where you are right now and miss out on some great opportunities.

James Allen, a British philosophical writer and the author of a book titled *As a Man Thinketh*, said, "All that a man achieves and all that he fails to achieve is the direct result of his own thoughts."[4] Following that logic, if you believe you will be a success, you will have success—or, if you believe you will fail, you will fail. What if you stopped for a moment, when some of these negative thoughts showed up, and questioned them? What if you realized that the thoughts were made up of others' beliefs and experiences—things that other people told you—and made the choice not to believe them? If you chose not to believe the negative thoughts, would it change what you did next? James Allen also said, "...the outer conditions of a person's life will always be found to be harmoniously related to his inner state."[5] Imagine what you could do if your inner beliefs changed. What if your thoughts were focused on what you wanted to create in your life instead of the old fears that hold you back?

Let People See Your Value

I INVITE YOU TO LET go of the negative thoughts about yourself that take away your energy. They will hold you back and no one will see you at your best. Imagine how you would feel if you took away the negative, self-doubting stories and replaced them with positive ones in which you succeed. A focus on what is possible gives you the confidence to be brave and bold enough to put yourself out there. I believe that anyone can shift their

Chapter 1

mindset if they put their energy toward it. I have done it myself. That doesn't mean that I am without doubts, but that I make a conscious choice to see a positive view instead. I want you to believe in your own capacity to make this happen. Trust that if you do the work, you can shift your mindset, too.

Do you think to yourself, *I could do more if someone would just tell me how*? I bet that, deep down inside, you want people to see you so you can show them what you can do. You want to sit at the table instead of at the back of the room. You want to progress in your career and rise to a higher level. You want to use your voice and have people listen to what you have to say.

The Visibility Factor and the process within will show you how to be seen in a way that is authentic to you, and I will be right by your side as your virtual coach. You will learn how to make choices to be visible, and experiment with shifts in a way that is authentic to you and how you want to be perceived. You will create a plan based on where you are right now and choose from a list of tried-and-true visibility actions that have been used by me, my clients, and many of the leaders I have interviewed for this book. You will create a plan of your own that will put you in front of the right people and show your value.

You may be skeptical and think, *But I work harder than anyone else. Don't they already see my value?* Maybe they do, but not all of it. Let me use a movie theater analogy to explain. Your friend plans to meet you at the theater to watch the show. What if he runs late and only catches the credits? He's missed the entire movie, including all the good stuff. He has no idea what happened before he walked in. That is what happens for managers every day. They only see glimpses of your day and not the whole picture.

Most of them have the best of intentions, but they can't be everywhere at once. They don't have the time to watch the whole show. You have to put the highlight reel about you and your team in front of them, in a consistent way that works best for you. That is how they will know what you do and what your capabilities are for future roles. It is important that you are the person your management thinks of first when it comes to future projects or promotions. I made too many assumptions that my management would see what I did every day. Why should I spend the time pointing it out to them? I was stubborn and thought I knew better. I was wrong.

Maya Angelou, author of *I Know Why the Caged Bird Sings*, poet and recipient of the Presidential Medal of Freedom said, "Do the best you can until you know better. When you know better, do better."[6] That quote resonates so much with me. I didn't know any better. Though it was out of my comfort zone, I had to learn—the hard way—that it was important for me to be in front of decision makers. I had to give myself some grace; I grew up at a time when it seemed hard work was all you needed to do to succeed, but things changed and I didn't know it (or maybe I chose not to see it). I focused on the work and results, but I didn't talk about what I accomplished with anyone. I was taught to be humble. I felt like I would be known as a braggart if I talked about what I did, and I didn't want that. My hope is that you can learn from my mistakes and see that this is a great opportunity for you. I promise that you can be in front of decision makers in your own way, and it is so much easier than you think!

Chapter 1

What Does the Research Say?

Over several years, the Center for Creative Leadership did a study on the "Realities of Management Promotion" with three major companies. They found that in 73 percent of cases, the determining factor in a person getting a promotion was that the person had visibility with the decision maker. The study concluded that managers focus on the one candidate they know and trust who has the capabilities to do the job.[7]

Your leadership needs to be consistent so management throughout your organization can see you. When someone mentions your name, you want them to talk about the strength of your leadership and the contributions you have made. This may be hard to believe, but your management wants you to be visible. You have answers and a perspective that your senior management does not. Please don't underestimate what you know, or put them on a pedestal. They are humans. Treat them as though they are your equals. Be yourself and share what you know. From my own experience, and that of the leaders I have coached and spoken with, the research is right. If you don't take those opportunities to get in front of decision makers, you won't get the promotion or new responsibilities that you want.

After the feedback from Kathy, I had to find my own way to stay top-of-mind with my management team. It was all new for me and I wasn't sure where to begin. I felt a bit overwhelmed, but I watched what other people did to see how I could learn from them. I saw them take credit for their accomplishments and offer to take on additional projects or responsibilities to help them look good to management. How many opportunities did I miss out on to get in front of people for myself and my team? It wouldn't help to look in the rearview mirror to see what could have been. I had to take steps forward to change myself. Are you ready to do the same?

The Path to Transformation

I DID NOT ASK FOR help back then. I had long held the belief that you should solve your own problems, or your management would think less of you. (What is the old saying—"If I could go back in time, knowing what I know now"?) I didn't want anyone to see that I didn't have it all together. I thought that I needed to maintain the Sweet Perfect Sue image everyone had of me. I had not yet learned the importance of vulnerability and that it was okay to let others help me. This caused my transformation to take a lot longer. I compare it to a walk in the dark without a guide or a flashlight to help me figure out the path toward my own authentic way of being visible. In hindsight, I know that if I had allowed myself to be vulnerable and ask for more help, I could have shifted my perception much sooner. But at the time, I was worried about my optics with management and lived with the limiting belief that I needed to solve everything on my own.

Every time I attempted new actions to increase my visibility, my doubts would surface and hold me back. My perfectionism and fear of failure showed on a regular basis and kept me from taking those actions. *Do I have what it takes to be successful? Can I show others that I'm different?* As I said in the introduction, I am a huge reader. So I looked for books on how to overcome the fear and become more visible. I was sure that others had been through this and I could learn from their stories. However, I found limited information, so I knew it was time to ask for help from someone I knew had been through this before.

There is an old saying: "When the student is ready, the teacher will appear." This has been true in my experience. One day, an executive coach did a lunch-and-learn presentation for our IT group at Kraft. I knew that I needed a coach, but had not felt a connection with any of the others I'd met. This coach had a down-to-earth style, approach, and authenticity that led me to have another conversation with her. I talked to her about my situation and about the problem with how I was perceived. I hired her to help me get my confidence back and turn that perception around. In our first session, I created an action plan that would get me in front of my management team the next day. I felt so motivated and excited to try out these new ideas. Although it still seemed scary to move out of the background, I now had a coach in my corner who believed I could do it. My teacher had arrived to help me navigate the journey. Though I was still scared to make a mistake or fail, I borrowed her confidence in me to experiment with this new approach to stand out.

Empower Yourself

HARVEY COLEMAN PUBLISHED A BOOK called *Empowering Yourself: The Organizational Game Revealed*. He came to speak at our company and shared a presentation about his book. As I sat in the auditorium with many of my peers, I had a big aha moment. Coleman's message was that your success is based on your performance, image, and exposure, a.k.a. PIE. Performance is the day-to-day work that you are responsible for delivering. Image is how people see or perceive you, also known as your personal brand, and exposure is who knows about you and what you do. Up until that point, I believed that performance would drive the highest levels of success for me; my aha moment was that it is the complete opposite.

Coleman shared that "performance drives only 10 percent of success, image drives 30 percent and exposure drives 60 percent."[8]

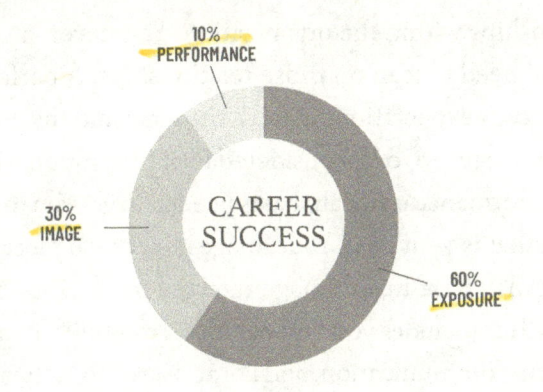

10% PERFORMANCE
30% IMAGE
60% EXPOSURE
CAREER SUCCESS

I couldn't believe that performance was only worth 10 percent of what it took for success. Now I understood why I had been stuck. I was focused on the wrong thing. I needed to move from performance to exposure, and I had to do it now.

Performance of your job is what we used to call "table stakes" at the company. This term comes from the gambling world. Table stakes is the minimum amount of money that you need to play poker. It is what gets you into the game; after that, you need to win so that you can stay in the game. In the business world, table stakes are equal to the capabilities you must have to get the job; to continue to work there, you have to perform well.

Your performance can be broken down into two parts: the what and the how. Think about the "what" as the things you deliver and accomplish as part of your role. The "how" is the way you work with others and the interactions that you have.

You may be great at what you do, but if you don't work well with others, it can diminish your work and give you a reputation for not being a team player. As you progress into higher-level roles, it becomes more important that you focus on your relationships within the organization. You never know when you will need to lean on those relationships. A performance that exceeds expectations in both the what and the how is the minimum needed to be considered for a promotion. However, your performance is not all that is needed to get you to the next level, if that is your goal. Your image is a critical piece as well.

You may have heard image referred to as "your personal brand." This includes your appearance, credibility, confidence, behavior, communication, and composure. To gather insights into your personal brand, pay attention to the compliments or constructive feedback that you receive. How does the feedback line up with what you expected to hear? What did you want them to say about you? For example, if you want to be viewed as bold, then you have to take actions to be seen that way. Show the capabilities that align with the role you want to increase your opportunities for advancement.

You may have performance and image handled, but your success may be limited without the third piece, exposure.

When the Student is Ready, the Teacher Appears

The goal with exposure is to find opportunities that will help others get a view of who you are and what you can do. Your involvement in different projects or activities may allow others to see new skills and capabilities that they may not have seen in you before. They need to see you in different environments and positions to know if they can envision you in future roles with more responsibility. This is one of the biggest areas to focus on for success. Remember the research you read earlier in this chapter about the top reason people are promoted? It is because they are visible to their management. Put yourself out there so your management can see the value you bring, and they will think of you when opportunities arise. GLOBAL

Exposure also means being bold enough to share your career plan with your management. How would you feel if you weren't considered for the perfect role because you never mentioned that you were interested? This is the time when you want to use your voice to ask for what you want in your career. It demonstrates your confidence in yourself and your initiative to drive your own career plan. It also creates the space to have a candid conversation if your manager doesn't feel that you are ready for the next role. This isn't an easy conversation, but a necessary one to help you understand what you need to change to be ready for an opportunity.

Doubt and Fear

You may also encounter the opposite situation. Everyone else believes in you and wants to see you move to the next level, but you don't believe in yourself enough to see that possibility. In my situation, everyone else had so much more faith in me

Chapter 1

than I had in myself. I was viewed as a success by others because of my hard work and performance, but I didn't believe that I was ready for the next step. No matter how well I did, I would diminish my success and find ways to attribute it to someone or something else. I had the opportunity to speak at a few technical and business conferences about the work we had implemented. Other companies sought us out afterwards to ask for advice on what we had completed, and we won awards internally and externally in the industry. I was interviewed by reporters for online articles after my presentations. I received the highest rating of my career on my performance review that year. Sounds impressive, right? It still wasn't enough to convince me that I was a success. I didn't take the time to celebrate my accomplishments. What was wrong with me? The belief that I was not good enough and my perfectionism needed to shift. My coach and I chipped away at my limiting beliefs and focused on my self-worth and the confidence that I had lost. I wanted to believe that I could change, but I was skeptical. It was hard for me to see that possibility.

At some point, I tried to blame my lack of career progress on someone else. I told myself a story that I worked hard; it must be someone else who held me back. It can be easy to fall into a victim role without realizing that it has happened. However, that story was false. I was the only one who had the power to hold myself back. If you are similar to me, the frustration is huge, because you know that you can do so much more. However, you can't seem to figure out how to get past the fear in your head that holds you back. I had to start with small steps, and it helped me shift my thoughts to see what was possible and move past the fear.

The RISE Visibility Framework

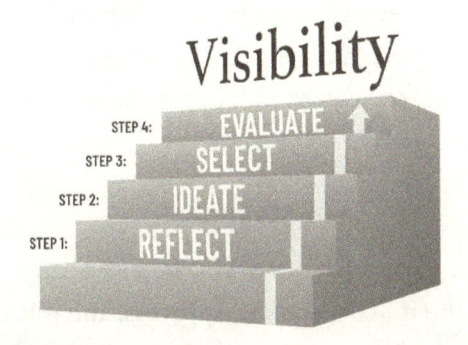

Visibility
- STEP 4: EVALUATE
- STEP 3: SELECT
- STEP 2: IDEATE
- STEP 1: REFLECT

WHEN I BEGAN MY JOURNEY to stop being invisible and stand out more, no checklist of steps existed for me to use. I had to build those for myself and create my own plan. I thought about what was needed to achieve the outcome that I wanted and created a list of questions to ask myself:

- What is my motivation to be visible?
- What do I need to do?
- How will I do it?
- How will I know if I am successful?

Over the years, I have refined these pieces into a framework that has four easy-to-follow steps. I named each step with a word that forms the acronym RISE to make it easy to remember. I picture it as a staircase that you climb as you complete each step to achieve the goal of visibility at the top. Although RISE is an acronym, I also see it as a metaphor. If you follow this method, you will feel empowered to rise above whatever has held you back from your goals. Everything that you do will help others see you in a new way. Your management will take notice and pay attention.

The RISE framework walks you through each step to help you create a unique plan that will work for you. You will learn more about the framework in Chapter 5, but here is a brief introduction to give you a preview.

REFLECT

Reflect is the initial step in the process, and it is necessary for you to assess where you are and why you want people to see you in a new way. This step allows you to figure out what has held you back and what your goals are. This is an opportunity to look at the possibilities that exist for you once you achieve the plan. My clients have shared that this step was one of the most impactful for them as they went through the framework.

IDEATE

The second step, ideate, allows you to generate ideas that you can use to raise your profile. I have created a list of ideas for you to review, but you may want to add your own. Observe what others do and what you can adapt to try out. This step gives you a creative approach to visibility and encourages you to be open to any ideas that will help you shine in front of management.

SELECT

The third step, select, helps you decide on the best ideas and actions and determines how you will measure your success. It is important that any idea you select fits your style and allows you to be authentic, but also pushes you out of your comfort zone. The details you include give you a game plan to follow to help you be intentional and focus your efforts each day.

EVALUATE

The last step, evaluate, helps you measure your progress. You will have captured feedback and other data to gauge your success with your plan. Assess the ideas that you implemented and their effects on how you are perceived, and modify as needed.

What Is Your Mindset?

You will have to make changes to old habits and start new ones, and that will challenge you to think in a different way and push you out of your comfort zone. If you follow the path laid out in this book, you will walk away with an actionable plan and the additional resources you need to raise your visibility. Your mindset is important to the achievement of success when you try something new and uncomfortable.

Let me show you a quick example of how your mindset can change your perception of an experience. I led our IT supplier management team at one point, and our outsourced teams for IT were in India. I was asked to attend one of our annual trips, but I was nervous to go there. I had not traveled with the senior executive team before, and I put them on a pedestal. Would I say or do the wrong things while we were gone? Would I get sick because I ate or drank something that I wasn't used to, as I had heard many others do? My coach asked me, "Can you look at the trip in a different way? Could you see how much fun it might be instead?" I never would have imagined that such a simple shift would change so much for me. From that moment on, I looked at the trip with a new perspective. I got excited about going! I loved the trip! I met so many wonderful people and learned so much about their culture. It was a once-in-a-lifetime experience that I will never forget, and I am so grateful to have gone there with a mindset of abundance and positivity.

If I had not shifted my mindset, I have no doubt that my trip to India would have been very different. What type of mindset do you have about your plan for more prominence? Are you excited or skeptical about what you will do and whether it will work for you? I ask you to be open-minded, or you will sabotage yourself before you get started.

Your Own Personal Coach

I KNOW THAT YOU CAN do this! This is a tried-and-true approach that I have used myself and now use to help my clients. I had to do this on my own, so I want to do what I can to support you as you go on this journey. Imagine me as your own personal coach to support you along the way.

With practice, your ability to promote yourself will become second nature for you and with each consistent action that you take, your confidence will grow. You will become the leader that you were meant to be, and everyone will see you that way.

I leveraged so many teachers to help me learn these lessons about visibility. I feel very blessed for the help that I received along my journey. It is my honor to pass on what I have learned

When the Student is Ready, the Teacher Appears

to my clients and now to you. It's time to let others know how great you are! Let's get started!

Actions

ARE YOU READY TO SHED the limiting beliefs that you have carried around with you? There is no need to hide or hesitate anymore! When you believe in yourself, your confidence will be apparent to everyone else.

1. I invite you to create a statement in the present tense that speaks to the leader that you want to be. An example could be "I am a visible leader" or "I am a bold leader." State it in the present tense so your brain believes it is already true. Write it down and put it where you can see it every day. Say it to yourself when you need a reminder of the leader you want to become.

When Kraft went through massive changes, there were so many unknowns to manage and make decisions on. It took my peers and me some time to learn how to be comfortable with being uncomfortable. We had buttons made that said, "Ambiguity Is My Friend!" You can't see anything that is your friend as truly bad, right? When we looked at it from that perspective, ambiguity didn't seem so hard anymore. We learned how to manage through it.

2. Can you think about visibility the same way we thought about ambiguity? Write down something that would make you uncomfortable to do, but that you could see in

Chapter 1

a new way and even have fun doing? Is there something that someone else does that you could adapt to your own style?

If you are ready to commit to taking your leadership to the next level and playing bigger, then join my Be Bold, Be Visible, Be the Leader You Were Meant to Be Facebook group![9] I can't wait to meet you and see you become the leader you were meant to be!

Uncomfortable things - new way stuff!
- *dinners with people.*
- *Small talk*
- *Presenting to others.*
- *Speaking in front of others.*
  - *→ not know it all by*
  - *Respond to questions.*
- *Host a meeting*
- *Team Building exercises*
- *Check-ins for no reason*
- *Networking groups.*

Write this - Put on desk - computer to see it everyday.

Notes

Leader you want to be.

I am a <u>visible</u> leader.

I am a <u>BOLD</u> LEADER.

I am a <u>GLOBAL</u> LEADER.

I am a <u>confident</u> leader.

I am a leader who <u>creates</u> strategy, <u>executes</u> through others, brings <u>others along</u>.

I am a leader who can manage through uncertainty.

Chapter 2:
FOLLOW YOUR OWN VISIBILITY PATH

AFTER I CHECKED MY MAKEUP in the bathroom for the third time, I told myself that I couldn't stall anymore. It was time to face my nemesis, the women's networking event that I'd come to attend.

When I entered the hotel for the event half an hour earlier, I saw a group of women seated at a table in front of the ballroom, welcoming attendees, asking us what companies we were from, and passing us our name tags. I looked inside the double doors behind the welcome committee and saw this huge room full of professional women in conversation with each other. Many of them had glasses of wine in their hands as they laughed and shared stories. The extroverts who walked in at the same time I did couldn't wait to get in there to meet people. They practically threw their coats at the hangers on the rack and ran in there. That is not how I felt, though. The thought of a room full of people that I didn't know made me feel nauseated. After the welcoming committee handed me my name tag, I asked where the restrooms were so I could stop in before I entered the room.

I may appear to be extroverted, but I am more of an introvert. It takes an enormous amount of energy for me to enter a networking session of any size unless I already know someone there. Is this true for you, too? I guess your answer to that question may depend on whether you get energy from big crowds or prefer to be with small groups instead. You might think, *How come this is so hard for her?* I understand how my hesitation must look to all my friends who love these events. They can't relate to it at all. They get so much energy when they meet other people. A room full of people is the perfect place for them and they love to be there!

If you don't know any introverts, let me share what happens for us. We would prefer to be at home in some comfy clothes while we watch our favorite show, enjoy a good book, or listen to music. We want to be anywhere that doesn't involve a bunch of people who want to talk to us. It isn't that we don't enjoy one-on-one or small-group conversations, but an entire ballroom full of people makes us feel overwhelmed. It takes every drop of reserve energy we have to put on our best smile and have conversations. We don't get energy in the same way extroverts do. We have to recharge our batteries by ourselves after any time with big crowds.

After I left the bathroom, I forced myself to go in the double doors and headed right to the bar. Can anyone relate? I grabbed a glass of wine (a.k.a. liquid courage) and checked out the appetizers... yes, I know that this is another stall tactic! I looked around the room for a small cocktail table where I could set down my wine while I ate my appetizers. I heard the critical voice in my head that I'd heard before, but it happened so often, I'd decided she needed a name.

Chapter 2

I nicknamed the voice Victoria. (She has a UK accent in my head, in case you wonder how she sounds.) She knew that there was some uncertainty here, so she pulled out the ol' introvert story and put it on repeat. *You know that introverts aren't good at this networking stuff and never will be. If you talk to people, you will be insecure and say things that don't make sense.* Victoria is a mean girl who is hurtful sometimes. *Why would you risk the judgment? Why don't you get out of here and head home instead? We can put on some sweats and read that new book that you got the other day. Wouldn't that be so much more fun than this?* Victoria was on a roll that night. I couldn't disagree. I was tempted to run out of the room, but it was too late. I was already there. I needed to stay and make the best of it.

Networking events always remind me of recess time on the playground back in grade school, when you tried to be included in whatever activity the group was doing and not to be a wallflower. The girls in my class did Double Dutch jump rope on the pavement at lunchtime recess. I wanted to be a part of the group and try it, but I had never tried it before. I didn't have the confidence that I could jump rope that way. *What if I make a fool of myself? What if they make fun of me or, God forbid, I fall in front of everyone?* One day, a girl from my class motioned me over to try it and showed me what to do. I was so grateful to her. Before I knew it, I jumped every day after that without fear. (By the way, in case you wondered, I got pretty good at Double Dutch and loved it!)

All right, you have stalled long enough, it's time to put on your big girl pants and go say hello to someone. I looked around the room and thought, *Who should I approach first? What will I say? Why didn't I plan this out more?* I approached a woman who looked nice and said hello to her. She said hello back and we had a good conversation. *Take that, Victoria!* This wasn't as bad as I made it all out to be in my head. I continued to network with five more people until it was time to sit down for the speakers.

On my drive home, I reviewed what had occurred at the event. I had created this story in my head that introverts aren't good at networking. That wasn't true, because I had just done it. I didn't have to talk to every person in the room; I only had to focus on one person or a small group at a time. That is what I am good at, and I can make choices about who to talk to and for how long. My preemptive fear of how the event would be was so much worse than the reality, and the story that introverts couldn't network made it easy for me to find excuses to avoid large-group events. If I let her, Victoria would keep me small and prevent me from the seizing the opportunity to try anything new.

This new world I had entered, figuring out how to put myself in the spotlight and promote what I accomplished, gave me the opportunity to look at what I knew with a new lens. It became clear to me that what I said and did needed to be intentional. I could no longer wing it and hope for the best when I met with people or attended meetings. I had always been quick on my feet, able to improvise and come up with responses, and perhaps leaned too much on that skill to get me through when I had to talk. I couldn't rely on that approach anymore. It was reactive, and I would have to be proactive from now on. It was a big adjustment to take the time to prepare and plan what I wanted to share with people. I felt better about what to do to prepare, but I also knew that this was only one piece of the puzzle that I needed to shift.

Chapter 2

Is Bragging the Only Option?

Now I HAD A PLAN for what I wanted to say, but how should I do it? I couldn't just walk into a conference room and say, "Okay everyone, pay attention… I have something to say, so get ready to listen!" Although that would have been funny coming from me, it would not help to create the image I wanted for myself. I struggled to figure out the best way to be bolder and yet remain myself. I only knew what everyone else did to get attention: they bragged. That was not my style, but I didn't see any other options. At the time, I had no idea that you could create visibility in any other way. In my heart, I feared I would have to become a braggart to get noticed.

Is there anyone in your company who brags to excess about their accomplishments while in meetings? I have met plenty of people who don't seem to know that they do this. It can become a habit that is hard for them to turn off. I assumed that the people who bragged tried to get ahead without any attempt to do the work. I only focused on the negative side of their behavior. To me, bragging and visibility were synonymous.

Any time I heard the word braggart, it triggered another memory of fourth grade. Do you remember Sister Loretta from Chapter 1? One day, she handed back the math tests that we had taken the day before. Math was not one of my best subjects, so I didn't expect an A. Many of my classmates didn't look very happy when they saw their test results. However, one of my classmates began to brag about the A he'd received on his test. I would have been thrilled to get that grade myself, but Sister Loretta wasn't about to let him go on about it when the rest of us didn't do so well. She told me and the rest of our class,

Follow Your Own Visibility Path

"Bragging about accomplishments is not something you should do." I could see his face fall when he had been so excited about his grade just moments before. She continued, "We should be humble about what we do and not make others feel bad." From that moment on, any talk about my own accomplishments became a negative thing to me, and I began to downplay my achievements. I am sure that Sister Loretta had no idea that her one sentence would have the power to change my beliefs, but it did.

Let me share an example so you can see why I thought that bragging was my only option. My leadership team and all my peers were in a huge conference room for a half-day meeting. There were twenty-five or so people in the room, each waiting to share their updates with our management. For many of them, this was a great opportunity to be in front of our senior management and share progress on projects. To me it was more painful, since I compared what I had done to what everyone else had accomplished. I spent a lot of time in comparison, and it was not helpful for me.

We had been told at the start of the discussion that there was a lot to get through, so we each had only five minutes to share an update. That amount of time was plenty long enough for me. I didn't want the attention of all these people on me any longer than necessary, so my plan was to get through it as fast as I could. I hit the key points without a lot of color commentary so I wouldn't go over the allotted time. I also wanted to give other people enough time. (Meet Sweet Perfect Sue, the people-pleasing good girl who wanted everyone to like her and followed the rules so she wouldn't get in trouble. UGH!) The person who sat to my right delivered his update next. He went on and on about how great his project was and how much of an impact it would make. No one said, "Hey, you are past your five minutes!" or, "We need to move on to the next person." Instead, our management team looked so proud and asked more questions. *Seriously? Why doesn't everyone see it?*

The Self-Critic

LET'S BE HONEST: THIS PEOPLE-PLEASING, rule-following belief system allowed me to hide and let others shine. Doubt and self-criticism were the loudest voices in my head. I listened to them and let them drive my decisions and behavior. The voices would say, *John is so much smarter than you, he knows so much more than you do. Mary has it all together, you can't compete with her.* I feared judgment from others but didn't listen to their feedback about me; instead, I listened to my own internal critic. I believed the stories that Victoria shouted in my head, and my actions reflected that. She said that I wasn't good enough and I should stay in the background. I believed it.

It is sad that I couldn't see any of this at the time, and it is painful to write about now. I held myself back and sabotaged opportunities because I didn't believe in myself. Is that something you have done to yourself, too? I made the decision to give other people additional time to talk rather than use my voice and share a longer update. Who does that? Someone who can't see their own self-worth and doesn't believe that what they have to say is important.

I thought that there must be another way to talk about the things that I did, but in a way that was true to myself. I wanted to stay safe and out of the spotlight. That was the easier path, but I soon realized it wasn't the path that would get me to my goal.

I didn't tell anyone, but I observed all my interactions with people from a place of deep curiosity. I saw them as test subjects for my own personal research assignment to understand what they did to talk about their accomplishments, so I could learn from them. I focused on what they said and how they said it. They had a natural ability to speak up in meetings and found ways to contribute information about their work as part of the conversation. They offered to take on additional responsibilities with such ease, I figured there must have been a class on how to do it that I missed somewhere along the way. They were masters, and I could see that I had a lot to learn. It became obvious that they created opportunities for these discussions every day. They took advantage of pauses in conversation to insert what they wanted everyone to know.

I sat in amazement as I watched and realized that I could learn from their efforts to stand out. It was a big shift for me when I chose to see what they did as positive instead of negative.

My little research project allowed me to capture ideas from these interactions and think about how I could use them in my own authentic way. I took notes of what everyone said and how they used opportunities to talk about their accomplishments. Some people found subtler ways to promote themselves and their teams. They looked for a problem to solve and then discussed how they could add value and solve it. They made it sound normal.

I had lumped everyone who talked about themselves into one group and called them braggarts. I had been so focused on my own self-righteous beliefs that I stereotyped them. I let my judgment of them cloud my view of what I could learn from them. I wondered if I could do something different that would work better for me. Could I find a way to adapt what they did and create my own approaches? This new possibility gave me the motivation I needed to experiment.

I shared my recent discoveries with my coach as we worked to unravel my old belief systems. All the beliefs I had been exposed to throughout my life, including what I learned from my parents, my friends, my experiences, and the environments around me, were under review. Some of these beliefs and stories were old and no longer served me. I could have filled multiple filing cabinets if I took them all out of my head and wrote them down. I hadn't been aware that I acted from old beliefs and stories, but now that I was, I could make changes. I had a choice to move on. I could let go of those old stories and beliefs to create new ones. It was time to let go of the old fourth grade story (sorry, Sister Loretta) and see that what I did to increase my visibility was good for me. I learned that when you take intentional approaches to increase your profile with others and share what you can do, you show them your value.

Be Your Own Advocate

My manager and leadership team were the people who made decisions about my career, my performance ratings and whether I would get a promotion. I had to be in front of them if I wanted to be considered for new opportunities. I could be stubborn, play the victim, and avoid situations where they could see my capabilities, but that wouldn't help me. I had to figure out how to advocate for myself. I put a plan together and found new ways to get in front of my management on a regular basis. I focused from that point forward with a different perspective. I found ways to stand out and look for opportunities to share accomplishments for myself and my team.

I had always assumed that my manager shared accomplishments and results with my leadership team on my behalf. Those conversations didn't take place. I don't know why I expected it to happen. It was naïve on my part and a good lesson for me to learn. You can't assume that your manager shares what you have done or will help you get the job that you want. Your manager may not be a good one, or know how to share their own accomplishments either. You need to take the lead and share what you and your team have done. It is an opportunity to build a relationship with the leadership team.

In my Create Your Authentic Visibility course, the participants were interested in ideas to help them get in front of their senior management. We discussed skip-level one-on-ones as an approach that works well. This means that you meet with your manager's manager for a one-on-one meeting. It allows you to be your own messenger, so you can share what you do, advocate for your career and build a stronger relationship with your senior manager in these discussions. One of the participants in the course had never considered this as an option before. She took the initiative to schedule a time to meet, created the agenda, and shared ideas that the organization could implement in her conversation with her CEO. She walked away from the conversation with higher confidence and a stronger connection with him. She was able to share information with him, but he also got to learn more about her and what she wants in her career.

Chapter 2

You Can Be Visible and Still Be Yourself

JOHN, ONE OF MY COWORKERS, was in many meetings with me and my peers. He had a reputation for talking a lot, but with little to no substance behind his words. Do you know anyone like this? When he opened his mouth, it was as if everyone would go into a trance. Our eyes would glaze over as we prepared ourselves to tolerate another lengthy monologue.

I always wondered how my management perceived John when he talked so much, sent out lengthy status reports and dropped by his manager's office all the time. Let's be honest: he managed up to his boss well. If he told his management a story that seemed credible in any way, they believed it. To those of us who knew the reality of the day-to-day, he was not credible, and his team struggled to get any direction from him. *Is that what it takes to get ahead?* It was hard for me to see him as a leader to emulate. What he did got him promoted. (I will add that it didn't change his reputation; he kept that with a fancier title.) I wish I could say this was an isolated situation, but it wasn't. It made it hard for the rest of us to respect the promotion process.

I never wanted the type of reputation that John had. I was resistant to talking about what I did for fear of any comparison to someone similar to John. It was important to me to remain true to myself and be authentic.

The Secret Decoder Ring

WHAT HELPED ME SHIFT MY perspective was a conversation that I had with Laura, who was a business mentor of mine. I

Follow Your Own Visibility Path

shared the feedback that I had received from Kathy. I told her that I needed help to understand what to do with the feedback now that I had it. It wasn't clear to me what Kathy meant and what actions to take. Laura offered to get out her "secret decoder ring" to translate what the feedback meant. She said, "Don't worry about what level you are at in the organization. You don't have to be a senior leader to make an impact. You do need to share what you know. You were hired for a reason and your senior management doesn't have all the answers or details about what happens in your team. They rely on you for that information, and they put you in this position to share what you know and add value. They want you to speak up and they will assume you have no information to add if you sit there without any involvement. Tell them what you think! They may not always agree with you, but they need your insights to help them make a good decision. That is what Kathy meant by visibility and why it is important for you."

As I listened to what she said, I thought, *Wait, what? People want to hear what I have to say?* I had judged my management team and thought they didn't want to hear from me. Of course I had information and ideas to contribute! They didn't judge me—I judged myself and created that story before anyone else could judge me. It justified my keeping quiet. UGH!! It is so hard to look back on that conversation and see how low my confidence was at that point. I didn't believe in myself at all. I didn't feel confident, but I knew I would have to start to say what I thought no matter how much fear I felt.

Laura continued, "Once you start, you will see that they will recognize you for what you have to say as a leader. They will look for your input and their perception of you will change."

Chapter 2

Do you believe that what you have to say matters? Trust me when I tell you that what you have to say is important, and you need to say it. Someone may talk about the one item you had planned to bring up, but don't worry—you can still contribute. You can ask a question that relates to what they shared. It is important that you get your voice out there and become more comfortable. There is no need to hide behind the stronger voices in the room. Their voices and opinions may be louder, and they may speak more often, but that doesn't mean they are smarter than you or that they are right.

My coach and I discussed what I had learned from Laura, my business mentor, to build an action plan. We talked about ways that I could do this authentically. She understood that I wanted to avoid the bragging approach that John and others had used. I experimented and took small steps to implement some of the changes. I started with the basics. I created questions to ask when I met with people, prepared specific points to talk about regarding projects, and put together a list of results that my team members had accomplished in recent weeks. My goal was to have these items ready when I saw opportunities to share them. This preparation was a good start, but I knew it wouldn't be enough to shift perception of me within the company.

I focused on these small steps in my interactions with anyone I talked to throughout the day. These small experiments helped me learn how to talk about myself. I got a little more comfortable with the new me who spoke in meetings. I began to see changes in myself that helped build my confidence. The experiments started to work, but I didn't stop there. I continued to add more ideas and approaches to ensure that I was consistent and out of my comfort zone. I knew that I felt different, but did others see it too?

I remember a senior management discussion that was a big deal for me. I asked a key question that brought about a much-needed conversation on the topic. As we discussed it, I shared my recommendation without hesitation. People listened to what I had to say. *What? I can't believe it! This stuff works!* The simple actions that I took began to change how people treated me in meetings and responded to me in conversations. This change in how I was perceived didn't happen overnight, but I was consistent and took small actions every day to move forward. None of this would have happened without Kathy, Laura, and my coach, who were brave and honest with me. Their feedback and advice shifted everything for me, and I am so grateful to these three women, who helped me learn what I needed to do to be seen. Although it was sometimes painful in the moment, their honest feedback was the best gift I could have received. It is now what gives me my purpose: to help you. I have taken hundreds of people through the same process that I followed, and I have no doubt that you can do it too.

What Does the Research Say about Visibility?

People in IT sometimes have a reputation for staying in their cubes and coding all day. Although that is true for some, many IT leaders do the opposite. We had some strong men and women leaders at Kraft who were great business partners and found ways to stand out.

Chapter 2

In 2016, Shelley J. Correll and Lori Mackenzie from Stanford University interviewed 240 senior leader technology professionals in Silicon Valley. They published an article called "To Succeed in Tech, Women Need Visibility" in *Harvard Business Review*, which I quote here: "They asked the group what is needed to be promoted to their level. A new top criterion emerged, eclipsing all others: visibility. More than technical competence, business results, or team leadership ability—these leaders agreed—visibility is the most important factor for advancement.

"In 2007 and 2008, the Clayman Institute for Gender Research and the Anita Borg Institute conducted research on approximately 1,800 tech workers in seven high-tech companies, finding that women reported being less likely than their male counterparts to be assigned to high-visibility projects."

Their results from various focus groups found that "visibility is a complex interaction of perceived skills (particularly technical and leadership ones), access to stretch assignments, and being known—and liked—by influential senior leaders within informal networks. All three are necessary for advancement."[10] A leader who doesn't fit the mold could be left out of consideration for high-exposure projects, opportunities to network, and the shortlist for promotions.

People tend to form cliques with their own groups or people who are "alike." Although the Clayman Institute research was focused on women, I believe that low visibility also impacts the underrepresented and men who don't fit the norm. They may be more introverted or struggle in social situations and have less of a chance of getting high-profile assignments. Some who are great but seen as different may be excluded from invitations to attend informal networking events. People want to belong, and when they don't feel welcome, their level of engagement goes down and they don't deliver the best results for themselves or the company.

One last challenge mentioned in the article is for people who have understated personalities. This trait can impact how both men and women are viewed. One person's performance review noted, "He is the most conflict-averse person I have met… this will be a limiter." Comments such as "He is too quiet," or "She doesn't participate in meetings" create perceptions that can be a challenge to overcome.[11] As a manager, you need to recognize the power you have to lift your people up or bring them down. The influence you have is larger than you may realize, and a casual, offhand comment about a team member to someone else can damage the perception of that team member. Every person has their own unique style, strengths, and gifts. A leader can build upon these traits and leverage the diversity of thought, perspective, and experiences in their team.

Even Introverts Take Risks

IN 2010, I TRAVELED TO Singapore for work with Kevin and Terese, my coworkers, and explored the city one night after dinner and drinks. We came upon a fun area of the city with restaurants and bars. Kevin said, "Look over there—they have a bungee jump!" He looked at me and exclaimed, "We HAVE to do it!" I had never bungee jumped before, but something told me to go for it. (As the saying goes, "When in Rome"—except, of course, I substituted "in Singapore"!) It was good that we

Chapter 2

didn't have to wait too long after I signed the release of liability, or I might have changed my mind. When it was our turn, we took off our shoes, emptied out our pockets, and gave all our belongings to Terese, who decided to stay on the ground to watch us. Kevin and I buckled ourselves in and looked at each other. This was a moment of excitement and a little bit of *What the hell are we about to do?* I said to Kevin, "I think I will have to hold your hand to get through this next five minutes." He was kind enough to do it—and then we soared into the air and back down again multiple times. It was one of the most exhilarating experiences I have ever had. It was a beautiful night, and so cool to see the city that way. (My children thought their mom was pretty badass when I told them what I had done.)

A second example was right before my team and I were supposed to go live with a new system that we had built in 2012. That day, we had a go/no go conference call while I was in the car on my way to the office. This go/no go call was a standard procedure to check in and make a formal decision whether to implement the system as planned. I asked my team on the conference call if there were any critical issues that remained to be fixed, and they said no. I remember the exact moment when I checked in with myself about whether I could see any reason to wait. I listened to my gut in these situations, and it had never steered me wrong. I couldn't think of any reason to delay. I told them, "We are a go, then!" Word had spread by the time I got into work. We were about to go live that night!

The next morning, I walked through the door and was instantly bombarded by some of my peers who had strong reservations about my decision. I listened to them and told them that I understood their concerns, but disagreed that we should have waited. It was a lonely moment, but I trusted my gut and knew it would be okay. This wasn't the first time that I had stood alone in a go/no go decision, but this one had company-wide implications if I was wrong, and the exposure could be big. I trusted my team and knew that they would walk through fire for me to fix the system if there were issues. Not every leader is lucky enough to have a team who could make miracles happen, but I had seen them do it. It wasn't a perfect launch—they never are—but overall, the implementation was viewed as successful. A few months later, at an off-site meeting, the IT organization gave me the "Run with the Bulls" leadership award. It is given to the person who isn't afraid to take big risks.

Both of those situations took courage and involved risks to my personal safety and to my career, but I trusted my gut and did them. How could I take these risks and still feel so afraid to put myself out in front of people?

Move Past Your Story

I REFLECTED ON THE DIFFERENCE between those situations where I took risks and those that I sabotaged. It occurred to me that the main difference was that, when I did risky things, I had people from my team with me. In a solo situation, I would find a way to sabotage myself and my opportunities. I had always put everyone else first and myself last. If I'm honest, it was easier for me. Since I was a child, I made sure everyone else was all right; that allowed me to be in the background. I didn't do this

Chapter 2

with any conscious thought, but I can see now that it was a way to keep myself out of the spotlight.

Have you thought about the stories or beliefs you may have in your head? Get out a piece of paper and write this down at the top of the page: "What are my stories or limiting beliefs?" Set a timer on your phone for five minutes and write down whatever your own personal critic says to you. Don't analyze or filter what you have written down. Look at the list when you are done and ask yourself these questions for each one:

- Is this story helpful or does it hold me back?
- Does this story prevent me from having the success that I want?
- Do I need to change this story or shift this limiting belief to a positive so it supports me instead?

Look at what you wrote down. What keeps you hidden? How can that be good? What if you made the choice to stand out 25 percent more?

My wish is for everyone to see the value they bring and be able to talk about it without any hesitation. It is key to have confidence, to be yourself, and know that you matter. You have gifts and strengths that others don't, and the world needs you to share them, not hide them. With the tools I will teach you, you can talk about the great results that you (and your team) have accomplished. It doesn't matter if you see yourself as an introvert or as someone who self-sabotages; you can do this.

I coach people on this every day, so trust me when I tell you that it is possible to move past these stories. I have done it myself, and so have my clients. Believe me, there is no need to compromise who you are for anyone or any role. You can be who you are. What you do doesn't have to be perfect.

When I coach someone, I help them see that they can take little steps to move forward; changes don't have to be big and dramatic to be effective. This truth gives people the permission to experiment. It frees them from their fear and boosts their ability to glimpse what is possible and try a different approach.

As I learned to shift my mindset about my limiting beliefs, it became so much more fun to do what used to make me so anxious. If you happen to be an introvert, know that you can be open with people and let them see you. Don't feel pressured to do what others do. You get to decide. This is what I love about this RISE visibility process that you will learn in Chapter 5. It creates the space for you to choose from a list of ideas and apply them in a way that works best for you.

Your Team Needs Visibility, Too

As you think about the action plan you will build, you'll want to include ideas and actions for yourself but also think about ways to gain exposure for your team if you have one. My lack of visibility hurt me, but also had unintended consequences for my team. They weren't in all the meetings with senior management to represent themselves; I was. They deserved to be recognized and talked about so that others knew how great they were. If I didn't share what they accomplished, there could be career implications for them. They trusted me to lead them and support them. I had to learn how to do this for myself and then teach them how to do it for themselves. It was time to push the birds out of the nest and teach them how to fly.

Chapter 2

I learned more about the new approaches that I could use to talk about results without the bragging. It was almost as if a fog had lifted and I could see what I hadn't before. I needed to teach my team how to do this, too! I had them "sit at the table" and make presentations to senior management. They were scared to do it, but I reassured them that they had every right to be there. They had conversations that they would never have had in the past. They used their voices and let people know that they were confident and as important as anyone else at any other level.

I continued to promote what they accomplished and taught them how to do the same for themselves. I watched them take actions that they didn't feel were possible before! These simple shifts changed the perception of my team and helped one of them land a role she wanted in the company, all because she became visible and promoted herself to others.

Visibility is important for you and even more important for your team. Your team doesn't have the same opportunities that you do to promote themselves, because they aren't in all the meetings that you attend as their leader. Take the opportunities, when they come along, to ensure that you promote both your great accomplishments and your team's. You should also encourage your team members to do this for themselves. They can start out small, in one-on-one conversation, and then progress to speaking in front of a group. When both you and your team focus on this kind of promotion, you can hold each other accountable to do more of it. It will shift the perception of you and your team in a positive way. You do great things and have fantastic ideas, but no one will ever know that if you don't tell them!

Follow Your Own Visibility Path

The actions I took were small steps to change how others saw me. That was important, but they also helped me see myself in a new way. I could see that people responded to me with different kinds of conversations, too. I saw my confidence come back a little bit more each day. I stayed focused and made sure that I set an intention each day to find ways to take new actions.

Every conversation I had at work was an opportunity for me to talk about what I or the team had done recently. It was easy to focus on the team, because I could direct attention toward them and not myself. My opinion could start to influence other people's opinions of my team members. I no longer saw this type of promotion as a negative; I saw it as a way to share the value that the team brought to the organization and to ensure that people knew what we did. We wouldn't be the group that no one had heard much about or didn't add value. That could be a death sentence to a group, and it could be eliminated. No—as I learned more about the importance of visibility, it became my mission to ensure that people knew that my group added value and supported our clients well.

Watching what other people did in meetings, I had learned how to take advantage of opportunities to show my value, and it kept what I did in front of my management. The people I observed created a positive perception of themselves in their managers' minds, and the minds of everyone else who attended their meetings. It was pivotal for me when I realized that I didn't have to brag. I could promote what I did in a way that was authentic to me. As someone who considers herself an introvert, I began to break down the walls of what visibility could mean for me and anyone else who struggled with it.

Chapter 2

Actions

SOME LEADERS DON'T WANT TO focus on the work they need to do to stand out because they see it as a huge mountain to climb. What if what you need to do is far simpler? What if all you need to do is have a conversation with someone else? Share a story about what you do, and they'll share theirs too. There is no pressure, and no specific outcome is needed. Every interaction is a chance to let that person know what you do, or your team does, and stay top-of-mind for any new opportunities.

If this is new for you, no worries. Here is a simple approach for you to try. (Note: number three on the list may take you a little more time to pull together, so start with numbers one and two for now. Add more stories when you are ready.)

1. Find opportunities to share what you and your team do with key people. If you are working in-person, you can have lunch, have a one-on-one, or see them in the hallway or elevator. If you are remote, schedule a thirty-minute one-on-one with them.

2. Here is a simple script to follow if you want to use it.
    a. "Hey, did you hear that _____? (Fill in the blank with what you want them to know—make this a thirty-second story).
    b. Talk about the impact that this had on the company or your group (cost savings, simplification, process improvement, etc.).

[Handwritten top-left:] Cathy the helped feedback my team - partnership

[Handwritten top-right:] - Current + Future Talent needs?
- FY25 Biggest Priority?

Follow Your Own Visibility Path

    c. End with a positive statement about or compliment for whomever was involved and worked on it with you.

    d. Ask them what their current responsibilities are so that you can learn more about them, too.

3. Prepare a few stories that you can use based on your work, so you are ready for any opportunity.

[Handwritten notes:]

Success
- VP ISC Leaders

Cathy - GBS, Finance, HR, (Director pool?)
Dorothy - Stakeholder w/ Beth -
inside search to outside? feedback.

c. Opportunities w/ Key people →
- Asger, ISC Leaders (3)
- Direct Source - Liberator. (GM)
- R+D, Introduce talent athlete - R+D leader - too big?
- Reduced agency spend. 50-75%
  2 yrs in a row
  yr 3

Cathy
Amy VP
Tralne
Alison VP HR

Shawn
- Mike G. EVPS
- Li al Byrd
- Mike Ford

★ Impact - Cost Savings ★
★ Experience Recruiting Sr. Leaders
★ Partnership increased w/ HRBP
Chris, Dorothy, Nicole, Emily, Caroline

Involve HRBPs

★ We have set up a VIP travel service for candidates.
☆

Notes

- have an Exec CRM ★
- have a playbook, standards
- Have HR on our team
- Have research capabilities
- Specialized model for high volume + high touch Sr. roles
- working on plan for pipeline requests, pilot now
- we reduced spend
- Reduced vendors
- terms w/ fee caps to protect us, limit expense
- We have Status Reports, branded
- we are working on telling the market story
- We advise, consult on the market
- we can leverage research firm for insel gathering

Future - we meet w/ internal talent — HiPos, talent conversations
- we are networking at NSN, XYZ conferences

Chapter 3:
ASK FOR HELP!

THE EMAIL SUBJECT LINE SAID, "WE ARE LIVE!" I read the email over one more time, to make sure I didn't miss any of the points I wanted to include before I hit send. It was a big moment—our IT project had just gone live! I took a deep breath and felt the stress leave my body. This program at Kraft had gone into production as the culmination of many months of work. The team and I were very excited that the go-live had gone so well.

On the afternoon of day one, I started to hear some complaints from our clients. They weren't happy about the new system. It didn't make sense to me, because I had their sign-off that they were good with the changes before we went live. I reached out to one of the business liaisons that we had on the project to find out why he thought our clients seemed so unhappy with the changes. His role was to prepare our clients for all the business process and system changes that would be impacted by the implementation of this new system. When I asked him why everyone was upset, he replied, "I didn't think that we would go live. I figured you would delay it, so I didn't

Chapter 3

want to waste the time to take them through all the changes." I could feel my blood pressure rise and my face turn crimson. *Don't lose your temper, Sue. Hmm... maybe I should say what I think in this situation... he needs to know how angry I am right now!* I took a deep breath and said, "But you told me that you had taken them through all the changes, and they were good." He continued to ramble on about how he was right to do this and blah, blah, blah. I couldn't listen to it anymore. *What the hell happened? I can't believe it. He took it upon himself to sabotage this. He did this on purpose, and tried to ruin this rollout for so many people. If we can't turn this around, it won't be his head on a platter, it'll be mine!*

This is what they call a leadership moment. You can play the victim or own what happened and fix the problem. I was beyond pissed off because I operate with transparency and integrity. *Who says that they will do something, doesn't do it, and then lies to my face?* I can't remember them now, but I am sure I had some choice words for him before I hung up. I would deal with him later. I had to take a few deep breaths and calm down. I pulled my team together to figure out a plan to address the issues with our clients. I knew my team would be angry that this had happened, too, so I had to stay calm. I wanted them to know that I would deal with it later, so we could work on the problem in front of us. I could point fingers at this guy who didn't do his job and blame him, but in that moment, it was all on me to ensure that we fixed the problem.

I was the person accountable for this program whether someone did what they were supposed to do or not. My peers had heard the news and wanted to talk about what had happened with our clients. I was pulled into a small conference

Ask for Help!

room by my peers, who also criticized my decision to go live. I couldn't believe what I heard! *Seriously? Anyone else want to come out to take some more shots at me, "share" their criticisms, and withhold support?* After about ten minutes in that conversation, I got a phone call from my daughter. I might have called her back in any other situation, but I was so close to tears that I needed to leave. I told my peers I had to take the call and walked out. No one had my back except my team. I was so grateful for them in that moment. It was supposed to be a day of excitement that my team and I could enjoy after all our hard work. The reality started to pull me down, and it felt horrible. I couldn't let my team see this, so I kept it all inside and put on the brave face.

My director approached me later that afternoon to see how the implementation was going. I gave him my best "everything is great" smile as I said hello, but I have no poker face. I am sure he had heard from other people that things were not perfect. He pulled me into an office and said, "How is it really going? What help can I give you?" Sweet Perfect Sue said, "We are good. Thank you for the offer, though, I do appreciate it." *I can't let him see that I don't have all of this under control or that I need him to bail me out on anything.*

"Sue, it is okay to ask for help, you know." My ego shouted, *No it isn't!* He continued, "I ask my VP for help all the time. You will be able to move so much faster and get new ideas if you do, too. I promise it will not reflect negatively upon you to ask someone for help." Until that point, I believed that I had to handle all the responsibilities on my own. I had grown up with the belief that you need to solve your own problems and that you are weak when you ask for help. It seems crazy when I look back on it now, but this was a core belief that I had.

Chapter 3

It was a pivotal moment to hear that I could ask for help and it wouldn't hurt my career. I thought about that one conversation all day. It released all the pressure that I had put on myself. I wanted to be perfect and appear to have it all together, but my director had just taught me that there was no need for me to do all this work on my own anymore. I didn't have to know all the answers, and that gave me the freedom to be a better leader. I could rely on my team to find answers, and work with them to identify the best solutions. I could tap into the knowledge of my peers and management for help. I felt so empowered.

I am so grateful to that director. He gave me the permission I didn't know I needed and helped me move past that limiting belief. I have shared this story with countless people to help them see that it is a lesson we all need to learn: Ask for help and you can move forward faster. It is a sign of strength, not weakness.

I also learned that there are times that you have to take a stand for what you know is right. It takes so much courage to do this when everyone else tells you that you are wrong. This was a big moment for me to trust in myself and my team. No one else on my team knew all the behind-the-scenes crap I had to deal with that day; it was my job to handle it so they could focus on what they needed to do. All they needed to see was that I had their backs and believed in them no matter what.

I believe that all the situations in our lives teach us what we need to know to prepare for what we will do next. All the lessons I learned helped me become a better leader then, and they help me coach my clients now. This book includes so many of those lessons for you to benefit from, too. Do you have any limiting beliefs that may cause you to struggle or be less of the leader you want to be? The awareness of these beliefs and how they can hold you back is a first step. Are those old beliefs still true? Do those beliefs serve and support you? Will they help you be the leader you are meant to be?

Byron Katie Can Change Your Thinking

IF YOU HAVEN'T QUESTIONED YOUR thoughts before, let me introduce you to someone who changed everything about how I understand them: Byron Katie. She is the author of multiple books that help people look at their thinking in a new way. I first learned about her when I read a book called *Loving What Is: Four Questions That Can Change Your Life*,[12] which helped me realize how much I craved external validation. I remember that after I finished the book, I said out loud, "Why didn't I read this book ten years ago?" It was one of those moments that I'll never forget. I had wasted too much time and energy trying to be what others wanted. I could stop the comparison and judgment that I lived with every day. I could trust myself and do what I thought was right.

Katie herself had been depressed for years, and found her way out of it through a self-inquiry process she created called "The Work." She now uses this same inquiry process to help others who have lived with stressful, sometimes traumatic experiences and thoughts for years.

This is how Byron Katie explains what she does on her website. "As we do The Work of Byron Katie, not only do we remain alert to our stressful thoughts—the ones that cause all the anger, sadness, and frustration in our world—but we question them, and through that questioning the thoughts lose

Chapter 3

their power over us. Great spiritual texts describe the what—what it means to be free. The Work is the how. It shows you exactly how to identify and question any thought that would keep you from that freedom."[13]

I went to see Byron Katie speak with my coach in Scottsdale, Arizona a few years ago. Katie is quiet, unassuming, and has a smile that reminds you of your favorite grandmother. Yet when she does "The Work" with people in the audience, she is unafraid to call them out with that same smile, especially if their thoughts keep them in victim mode. She wants them to move away from those thoughts that cause them to suffer. That day, I watched her help multiple people in the audience who had experienced severe trauma. Katie had heard similar stories before, but I felt uneasy. It was uncomfortable to witness as others shared the personal, tragic situations they had survived. Many of these tragedies had occurred when they were children, and they relived them every day. I had so much compassion for what they had gone through and continued to experience. They came to see Katie that day because they had already been in therapy for years and felt that she was their last hope to rid themselves of their painful thoughts. Katie helped them see that those situations from so many years ago were not actually happening in the present moment, yet their actions in the present were filtered through a lens of fear that the trauma could happen again. She wanted them to realize that they were safe in the present, and what happened to them in the past could no longer hurt them. It was their thoughts about the past that caused them to suffer now.

On the plane ride home the next day, I thought about the deep personal conversations that I had witnessed. How do

Ask for Help!

humans relive the past over and over without the knowledge that they are living in the past and not the present? I began to look at multiple situations where I'd felt wronged in the past that I had projected onto a person or a new situation in the present. My pride had been hurt back then, and I couldn't seem to let go. After this experience with Byron Katie, I could see that it wasn't good for me to hold on to the old experiences anymore. I needed to do the work that Katie shared to forgive myself and others in each of those circumstances. It was time to get rid of the negative, old stories and move on.

Is there an old situation that you haven't let go of yet? What if you could use "The Work" process and help yourself move past it? This may not be the traditional way for you to get help, but if it works for you, isn't that the important part? Is there a circumstance or person that makes you feel upset or frustrated right now? If it is helpful to you, go to Katie's website,[14] download the "Judge Your Neighbor" worksheet and try her process. I've found it useful when there is an issue between two people and one of them cannot let it go.

You don't always need the other person to be involved to move on. If you have tried to work it out and they are not interested, you can do this on your own. You get to decide if you want to shift your viewpoint and choose to let go. I have seen experiences from the past play over and over in others' heads and in my own. Take the time to look at this episode from a different angle. You may discover that you had a role in what occurred that you couldn't see before because it was easier to blame the other party. What if this situation that happened so many years ago is the reason you don't put yourself out there and do more? You may have the fear that it will happen

Chapter 3

again, and so you take no action. It's time to let go of whatever from the past holds you back from what is new. What if the other person was innocent? People's actions are driven by what they know and believe. Could the other party have been misinformed, made assumptions, or made the best decisions with the information they had in that moment? Forgive yourself and the other person, and let it go. If I can do this, I know that you can, too.

A Little Help from My Friends

I DECIDED THAT I WANTED to try to get in shape after I had my second daughter, Kelly. She had been born a few years earlier, and for the first six months I didn't get to sleep much. I was happy that I could match my clothes before I went to work, but I had no energy to exercise. (I am sure anyone who is a new parent can relate.) Everyone I worked with ran, and it was a big topic of conversation each day at lunch. I didn't have anything to contribute on that topic; I had run to work out, but not in races. I heard my coworkers talk about the different races they signed up for and the runs they had to do each week to train. They didn't compete against each other, but focused on improvement of their own times instead. They made it sound so positive and fun to be a part of the race experiences. *Could I do this too? Could I run the half marathon they plan to run?* I am logical, and started to go through the decision model in my head to come to an answer. I used to run for fun in college, so I assumed I would be able to handle the shorter races. *Could I train enough to complete the full distance? Yes—I will run shorter races to prepare for the longer ones. Do I have the time to train for*

Ask for Help!

the races? The training and races will be on the weekends, for the most part, so I won't have to take too much time away from the family. I had the answers that I needed.

I announced at lunch one day that I planned to run the Indianapolis 500 Festival Mini-Marathon next May. There were no camera crews around to tape this big moment, as there were when President John F. Kennedy made the bold statement that the United States would land on the moon. I suppose his statement was a bigger deal compared to my run in a half marathon race, but I hadn't yet completed a 5K at that point! I had always set big goals and then figured out how to get there. I knew I could do it, plus I had these "experts" around that would help me. My friends shared resources that I would need to build my plan to run. We talked about the races that they had signed up for so I could decide if I wanted to join them. I was excited about this new adventure. My friends knew way more than I did, so I wouldn't be alone. I would learn a lot from them. The more we talked about it, the more I could see myself crossing the finish line!

My friends ran with me to keep me motivated. I joined them for multiple shorter races that fit into my plan. This gave me shorter milestones to focus on and build upon toward the big half marathon goal. Some of those races went better than others, but my goal was to improve and adjust my training as needed.

My sister, Debbi, lives in the Indianapolis area, so I asked her if she wanted to run the half marathon with me. She used to run cross country in high school and pulls out that old experience when she needs it. I had followed the plan as if it were a recipe, so I was a bit jealous that she didn't have to train as much as I did. The 500 Festival Mini-Marathon was held in preparation

Chapter 3

for the big Indianapolis 500 car race, which also happened each year in May. That first Saturday in May at 7:30 a.m., all the runners assembled in downtown Indianapolis. We stood in our corrals, metal gates labeled with letters assigned based on our estimated pace. The corrals were divided up by the fastest times at the front to the slowest times at the back. I was nowhere near the front among the twenty thousand people who had prepared to run their best race times that day. I was excited and nervous to stand with all those runners; I had stepped out of my comfort zone and completed what I said I would do, and now it was time to run the race!

The temperature was cool with no wind, perfect to run in, but as the sun came out, the temperature began to climb. As we approached the halfway point, we entered the Indianapolis Motor Speedway to run a lap on the two-and-a-half-mile loop. It was a bit surreal to run on the track where I had seen cars on TV eclipse 225-plus miles per hour. It takes them forty seconds to drive a lap around the track. It took me a lot longer to run it! The track has no shade whatsoever, and it was eighty-five degrees out. My sister, my friends and I began to see people drop out of the race because of the heat, but we didn't stop. When we crossed that finish line, I was beyond exhausted and so happy that I had made it! I was by no means the fastest runner in the field of participants, but I had achieved a huge goal! It was my first big race, but it was special to have run the race with my sister and my friends. We have a picture of us with red, sweaty faces and our finisher medals around our necks. It is such a great memory, and such a big goal achieved.

I share that story with you as an analogy to the journey you are about to go on. You don't just get out of bed one day and

Ask for Help!

run a half marathon without much training (unless you have the running gift my sister has). You have to set a goal, and it takes time to move from beginner status to a more advanced stage. There will be ups and downs as you "train" for this new way to communicate, but you will cross the finish line with new skills to leverage.

What goals do you want to achieve in your leadership and career? Are you ready to start this journey now? This decision is no different than mine when I decided to run the race. I needed to remind myself that this was a goal I wanted to achieve for my health, and I asked for help from people who knew how to train. This book was written to help you understand why visibility is important for you, to give you the steps to stand out, and support you through your journey. You will not be alone. You will have me and a community of people who are on the same path with you. Connect with the community: join the Be Bold, Be Visible, Be the Leader You Were Meant to Be Facebook group.[15]

Are there people in your world who could support you at work or at home? Would they help you? Perhaps this is a journey you could take together and help each other succeed. I encouraged the participants in the Create Your Authentic Visibility course to think of ways to support each other. Here were a few of their comments about what helped them the most:

- "Having an accountability partner, someone who can help provide immediate feedback on my visibility or lack thereof during key meetings and in interactions with team members… I was much more proactive,

Chapter 3

and continued to remind myself that I needed to make my voice heard and contribute to meetings versus just sitting back, taking random notes and multitasking. My accountability partners have been very kind, but when they see me falling back into my quiet zone, they nudge me for feedback or input during meetings."
- "Getting feedback from peers and other leaders. Taking a step back and thinking about exactly what I want and putting a plan in place for how to get it."
- "This has helped me realize that it doesn't have to be so complex. If you are being mindful of trying to be visible, then you pay attention to opportunities as they present themselves—an opportunity to speak in a meeting, an opportunity to call out someone else on the team for doing a good job. While making bigger moves certainly gets you visibility, there are a lot of smaller things that you can do if you are just being mindful."

As you can see by some of these comments, the shift to create more visibility is a process. It doesn't happen overnight, and you need help from other people to speed your progress and see results. Commitment, consistency and intention are the secret weapons that will help you cross your goal finish lines. These new actions will challenge you at first and take you out of your comfort zone. But, just as if you were training for a race, you will figure out what works for you and it will become easier. Your commitment to focus each day on your goals will make people see you in a new way. I have taught so many leaders to do this, and I know you can do it, too.

Don't Be Afraid to Ask for Help

I WOULD NEVER HAVE BEEN able to achieve my half marathon goal if I hadn't asked for help from my friends. They were an invaluable resource for support, guidance, and clarity in helping me see that I could do this when I wasn't sure of it myself. It is important that you enlist others to support you as you begin to make changes. Ask for help from friends, trusted advisors, managers, peers, mentors, sponsors, and coaches. They are the people who know you the best and can give you honest feedback.

Remember how important my mentor, coach, and business mentor were to my transformation in Chapter 1? They were the three people who were honest with me. They changed how I saw myself and the actions that I took. Without their help, I wouldn't have been able to move past some of my biggest challenges.

Do you have a mentor or a sponsor? I get a lot of questions about the difference between a mentor and a sponsor. How do you decide the best one to leverage and when?

Mentors will share their experiences and career lessons with junior- to mid-level leaders, but will also help other leaders who may need their guidance. They can help future leaders with high potential see situations and people in a new way and provide support with challenges. A piece of advice for you when you look for a mentor: Identify someone who demonstrates the skills or has been through the experiences that you want to cultivate or pursue. Don't choose someone who is similar to you. Find someone who can show you different ways to take action and shift your perspective so you can break out of your normal practices. It can be a formal mentor relationship, or it may just be a few informal conversations that will help you get what you need. Mentors are also always on the lookout for people in the organization who are top talents, so someone may approach you. That is a great sign that they see your potential. The bottom line is that a mentor can give your learning and growth a big boost.

Sponsors are senior-level executives who have a lot of influence and can help to advocate for you. They can put you into high-exposure roles and lend you their support in promotion discussions. There may be a more formal process to get a sponsor, because it is a big commitment for a sponsor to take you on. The sponsor will vouch for you and lend you their credibility. If they place a bet on you and you do well, then they win, too. If you struggle and don't listen to their advice, it can be difficult for them to move past that situation, too.

You have to be all the way in to the partnership when you work with a sponsor. The yes you give them sends a message of commitment that you are ready to move as fast as you can. Make sure you are committed before you say yes, and work with a sponsor only when you are ready to jump in with both feet.

By the way, you can have the support of both a sponsor and a mentor at the same time. A mentor may be there to help with a specific business or team situation, but a sponsor is there to help you accelerate your career. In most cases, a sponsor relationship is built over multiple conversations, and they will make the decision to go forward with you—or not—based on what you want and how you handle yourself. Some organizations have a more formal process for sponsor relationships, such as the one IBM Europe created to help women advance.

Ask for Help!

A *Harvard Business Review* article written by Herminia Ibarra, Nancy M. Carter and Christine Silva, "Why Men Still Get More Promotions than Women," discusses how the model that IBM Europe uses to drive accountability is intended to help women get visibility in their organization. "To reap the benefits of sponsorship, companies must hold sponsors accountable. At IBM Europe, a sponsorship program designed for senior women below the executive level aims to promote selected participants within one year. Sponsors, all vice presidents or general managers, are charged with making sure that participants are indeed ready within a year. So, they work hard to raise the women's profiles, talk up the candidates to decision makers, and find the high potential internal projects that will fill in their skills gaps and make them promotable. Failure to obtain a promotion is viewed as a failure of the sponsor, not of the candidate."

This is a unique approach that puts a high level of accountability on the sponsor. It ensures that they are invested in the success of the person they sponsor and that they don't just go through the motions. The authors' overall conclusions showed that this type of program isn't all that is needed, however.

"More sponsoring may lead to more and faster promotions for women, but it is not a magic bullet: There is still much to do to close the gap between men's and women's advancement. Some improvements—such as supportive bosses and inclusive cultures—are a lot harder to mandate than formal mentoring programs but essential if those programs are to have their intended effects. Clearly, however, the critical first step is to stop over-mentoring and start accountable sponsoring for both sexes."[16]

Chapter 3

Do You Have Trusted Advisors in Your Corner?

IF YOU DON'T HAVE ACCESS to a mentor or sponsor—or even if you do—you can also identify people in your life to be your trusted advisors. Everyone needs a trusted group of people in their life whom they can rely upon for honest advice and feedback. Select four to six people who will provide a perspective that is different than your own. You want members of your advisory group to be people you can trust to provide support when you need to make big decisions.

Advisory groups can help you gain new perspective on yourself, point out blind spots or remind you of your past accomplishments that are relevant to your current decision. Here is a good example of when to use an advisory board: A recruiter reaches out to you to take on a VP-level role at another company. The role has a higher level of responsibility than you have had before, and you can feel the critic in your head tell you that you're not ready and you should turn it down. If you listen to the negative thoughts, you will choose to stay where you are. This is an illustration of "playing not to lose" versus "playing to win." Big decisions bring on the doubts, and a new role comes with the fear that it will push you too far out of your comfort zone. Your advisory board is there to assist you as you think through your options and help you make the best decision for you. They are there to support you, not to make the decision for you.

I interviewed one of my former mentors and advisors who climbed the ranks to the C-suite in multiple companies and geographies. He is well known for developing people and for his visibility in social media. I was curious to understand how he thinks about visibility and what he advises others to do. He offered four suggestions: "The first thing is to get visibility externally as early as you can, which puts pressure on your internal management to pay attention to you. Next, understand yourself and what you have passion to do. What brings you energy may be things that are inside or outside of the office, with your community and with your family. Focus on those things. The next piece of advice is to not live up to your job description. The day you live up to your job description, you're limiting yourself for no reason. For example, what if I look at my team as the 100,000 employees of a company? There are no limitations to my team. What can we accomplish? Lastly, if you focus on the intersection of your passion, without the limits of a job description but with an unlimited team, you can do amazing things."

Can a Coach Help Me?

I AM BIASED, SINCE COACHING is what I do, but you have read my story. You know that I was a client at one point—and still am, with my current coach—and that the experience of coaching helped me to see myself in a new way. It gave me confidence to deal with the things that I was afraid of and challenged me. I know what a difference a coach can make for a client who is navigating a difficult situation.

Let me share an example of how coaching helped one of my clients. Maria struggled to get some of her clients to align with her on project deliverables. She had been at the company for about six months and thought her manager might have more insights to share on why the clients weren't aligned with the plan, so she asked him for advice to help her solve the problem. He told her she would need to figure it out, talk to them, and get them on board. She struggled to read him. Would this conversation create a negative perception of her? The conversation reinforced the self-doubt she felt because she was new to the company.

It wasn't the first time she had tried to talk to him about her difficulties without success. The transition into her new job had proved to be a challenge. Maria felt as if her manager had no confidence in her abilities, so after this, she didn't ask him for help anymore. It seemed as if she couldn't do anything right, and when she talked with him, he made her second-guess her decisions.

Maria hired me to be her coach about six months after she started at her new company. As we worked together, she shared some of the situations that she faced with her coworkers. She struggled to advocate for herself and often let people be disrespectful to her. She couldn't seek out her manager's advice anymore and needed to find a way to move forward with decisions without her manager's input. We focused on ways that she could stand on her own, make decisions with confidence, and build stronger relationships.

I wanted her to think about why she felt she needed her manager's input. We talked about what she could decide without him, how she would have handled a similar situation at her old company, and if there were people in the organization she could leverage when she had questions. As we talked, she began to see that the insecurity she felt was driven by fear. She wanted to do well and not fail in the new company. I asked

Ask for Help!

her, "Do you think your manager's approach to push you into finding your own solution will help you?" She said, "After this discussion, I can see that my manager trusts me. He wants me to learn how to do this for myself, be able to build relationships with the team, and face the conflicts with the team."

Each coaching session was an opportunity for her to discuss a situation, identify some alternative ways to handle it, and role-play with me to help her develop a bolder voice. Her confidence grew as she took bigger actions in front of her peers and her manager. There was still one person in her group with whom she struggled to build a bridge. We discussed different approaches to their conversations that might help Maria focus less on deliverables and due dates that caused friction and more on the person. The next day, she spent more time with her coworker to try and understand what caused them to feel defensive. This helped her understand her coworker better and develop compassion for their situation. Maria and her coworker built a stronger relationship and agreed on how to communicate in a better way.

About three months later, Maria put together her development plan. I reviewed it with her and then she went through it with her boss. He gave her feedback that she had made great strides in the last three months. He was impressed that she had done such a thorough job on her plan and had hired a coach to help her. He was supportive of her future career plans and looked forward to her continued growth. He approached her a few months later and asked her to lead an area of the company's new transformational initiatives. Her ability to step into a bolder voice and advocate for herself showed her manager that she was a strong leader, and it changed his perception of her. This experience helped Maria see how important it is to build relationships when you move to a new company.

Tap into the Wisdom of Experts Who Have Been There and Done That

WHEN I STARTED MY BUSINESS, the same fear and doubts arose. I had learned how to be visible in my old company, but now I had to figure out how to do it again, in a different way. This overwhelmed me and brought back similar moments when I had struggled at Kraft. I had to remind myself: *I have been through this before, I can figure it out.* I was on my own when it came to figuring out how to shine a spotlight on me and my business, though. I told myself a story that I didn't have the credibility I had before. I used to be able to introduce myself as part of Kraft, a company that had an established, high-quality reputation which translated to me because I worked for them. I benefited from that built-in trust. How would I establish that type of credibility for myself now?

I followed the list of "shoulds" that I thought all business owners checked off when they got started. I spent hours deciding on a name for the business, created the perfect website and— let's not forget—I found a logo online that I redesigned and made some business cards. I am sure I would have gotten an A-plus in the What to Do When You Want to Start a New Business 101 class! As I look back on all I did, I see that it was my attempt to establish a real business. I imagined that if these foundational items weren't in place, someone would question my legitimacy. I did take steps toward higher-exposure activities, such being a guest on podcasts. This allowed me to share my

Ask for Help!

insights with people on the transition from working a corporate job to entrepreneurship, leadership, and what I believe about coaching. My hope was that my podcast appearances would start to get my name out there and bring me clients. Podcasts scared me to death at first, but then I grew to love them. I started to be more comfortable with the uncomfortable.

I knew that entrepreneurship would challenge all my insecurities, but I was confident that I could push through them. I wanted people to see me as a coach and a thought leader in a field that was different than where I came from. They wouldn't hire me if they didn't know who I was or what I stood for.

Everyone has to decide for themselves what options are right for them to cultivate visibility. Start with whatever you feel passionate about and gives you energy. My choice was to write a blog. I had never done it before, but I watched another coach friend of mine who had done it with success. He encouraged me to write just one blog post. It took me an entire week to edit that one post over and over to determine if it was good enough (Hello, Perfectionist Sue), and still I hesitated to hit the button and send it out. It was time to be bold (it wasn't very bold in the big scheme of things, but it felt that way in the moment) and put the blog out to my email list and social media. I felt excited and scared at the same time! I'm not sure if I expected all kinds of feedback right away, but it didn't happen. I got a few likes, and that was nice. I knew that it would take time and I had to be consistent.

I have now written over eight hundred blog posts; I can focus and write each one in less than an hour. Everything becomes easier the more practice you have. I have found that the posts that I worry aren't good enough and feel most vulnerable about are the ones that I get the most feedback on.

The requirement is that you be yourself—the real authentic you, not the "social media perfect" version. Everyone can see through you when you aren't authentic. If you decide to use some form of social media to expand your personal brand, just be you and share what you have to say with the world. Just start somewhere and accept that it will be perfectly imperfect.

Actions

1. What are the limiting beliefs you discovered about yourself? Can you write down a positive way to reframe them so you can move forward?

2. Can you create a list of the people who are in your corner and support you no matter what? What could they provide to you that will help you the most (accountability, support, honesty, advice)?

Notes

I calculate the risks, strategy and actions before I decide to do something

You are cautious, helpful, kind.
You care about others, their feelings

You can count on me and my word, what I say, I will do. — My commitment level is high, I am loyal, I will do my best with what I have, I don't have to be perfect.

Move forward w/ other people do care about me + want to see me so they know how I can help.

Other people need my expertise,
other people need my team,

My corner:
 J, K, Nicole, Patrick,

Accountability to
Flower??
Danielle

Chapter 4:
THE INVISIBLE CHALLENGE OF VISIBILITY

I HURRIED INTO THE ROOM, stopping short once I got through the doorway and realized I was the last one to arrive. The entire room of twenty people all turned to look at me. *Yes,* I responded to them in silence, *I know I should have gotten here earlier.* I tried to avoid the spotlight, but that is impossible when you are the last person to show up. I scanned the conference room for an empty chair. *Seriously, Sue, why didn't you get here earlier?*

Deep inside, I knew why I wasn't there earlier. I didn't want to go this meeting, but I had no choice. I was the face of a global program I led, and that meant I had to provide updates to multiple groups in the company. This program was my baby to take care of and watch over, and these conversations were tough because everyone had an opinion about what we should do. Each session was filled with questions and criticism as my coworkers tried to call my baby ugly. I was sure that this meeting would be one of the most difficult yet. This group represented all the business units, and my program would change a lot of current business processes for their clients. They would not only have to buy into the program, they would also have to become

The Invisible Challenge of Visibility

my advocates and help me sell it. If they didn't agree with the program, I would be in real trouble, unable to move forward.

The meeting was held in a conference room just one floor down from my office. I had taken the back stairs as a shortcut to be there at least somewhat on time. The walls of the stairwell were painted gray, and that reflected how I felt as I made my way downstairs. I dreaded this meeting, and I might have taken my time to get there.

I wasn't a big fan of conflict, and I could feel the tightness in my stomach increase as I took the last available seat. It was directly across from the manager of the team. Her name was Lisa, and she always seemed to look mad. I don't think that she was mad; maybe a better description would be serious and intense. I knew Lisa, but had never presented to her or her team before. The room was cold when I walked in, and it felt like a sign that the group would be unreceptive to what I had to say. I put up my invisible armor and mentally prepared myself for a lot of pushback and tough questions.

Lisa smiled at me and gave me a warm introduction to her team. *I am confused. Is this a trick? She smiled at me.* I noticed that the cold air in the room had dissipated and it felt warmer. I hadn't started the presentation, and yet I already knew that I had her support. I could feel my invisible armor come down. *What is going on here?* I hoped my face did not betray the surprise I felt. I reviewed the plans for the program and got full agreement from her team.

Everyone else left the room at the end of the meeting except Lisa and me. I thanked her for her support and time. She shared that she had concerns about this type of program as it existed a few years ago. (A similar program had been tried before, but without success.) She told me that before I came into the room, she decided that she would clear those concerns away and listen to what I shared as if she had no previous judgments at all. *So that was what I felt!! I could feel her support for me from across the room.* What she did helped me to be successful and keep her team open to what I shared. She taught me what could happen when you remove judgments toward a situation or another person and give them the chance to shine.

Self-Sabotage

I WAS THE QUEEN OF self-sabotage and didn't know it. If you aren't familiar with the term, self-sabotage occurs when your behavior undermines your progress toward your goals. Did you see where I tried to do that when I had to meet with Lisa and her team? I could have been at that meeting earlier, but I took my time and arrived late. I tried to sabotage the situation to stay safe and avoid the fear I felt that the meeting might not go well. Logically, it made no sense. It put me into an awkward position and in the end, there was no reason to do it. It worked out okay in that situation, but many others didn't go as well.

Sometimes I would start one of the actions on my plan and then stop myself. I was so frustrated! *I know what to do, why don't I do it?* I could implement multimillion-dollar programs, but I couldn't figure out how to get past my fear and step up to the front of the room. It was an invisible wall that I couldn't break through. This unbreakable wall was comprised of my own fear.

What the hell was I so scared of? Success? Failure? Judgment? Comparison? I thought that once I learned what actions to take to be visible, it would be easy; but fear took over and I was unprepared.

It is important that you know about this challenge in case you find yourself in a similar place where you can't seem to move forward. I couldn't see my own value. I dismissed and rationalized to avoid taking any actions that might change the opinion I had of myself. I wanted to stay in the background and under the radar.

Resistance is especially big when you try out something new that pushes you out of your comfort zone. It makes you feel anxious, fearful, and unworthy. Resistance to these emotions seems too hard to overcome, so the response is to stop yourself from acting and then justify why that is the right approach.

Brad Yates, speaker, author, and coach, describes self-sabotage as "misguided self-love. That fear and resistance—generally based on old misunderstandings (yours or someone else's)—stops you from being, doing and having what you really want."[17] If we look at self-sabotage as a simple misunderstanding based on our mind simply trying to keep us safe in that moment, we can start to shift those thoughts and replace them.

It is clear to me now that I used self-sabotage as a protective mechanism to take myself out of the game before I could fail or be hurt. The beliefs were my reality at that time, and they created blind spots. Has this happened for you? What do your beliefs tell you about yourself? If you look at your beliefs and your thoughts in more detail, you may see things that you have not seen before. If your thoughts and beliefs don't support you, they could cause you to take a detour from the journey you want to be on and the goals you want to achieve.

Chapter 4

The Power of Stories
(or Are They Fairy Tales?)

As a reminder, stories are those thoughts made up of your assumptions, beliefs, and experiences. These stories are the lens through which you see the world.

I have always battled with the stories I told myself. I didn't understand how thoughts worked, so to me it was just my reality. My struggles make sense now, because I have learned that thoughts drive behaviors and actions. I didn't question my thoughts, and I underestimated how powerful thoughts and the stories you tell yourself can be. They can either help you move forward or keep you stuck in place.

I don't want you to hold yourself back and miss out on an opportunity to step into a new role, so let's dive a bit deeper into the stories and beliefs that existed for me so you can see some examples. As you read through these next few sections, notice if similar stories are happening for you, too.

In my own case, I learned that I had a bunch of these fairy tales in my head that appeared to be true but were false after all. I wanted the "Cinderella" happily-ever-after (I already had the prince—my mom used to call my husband Prince Charming; I wanted the promotion!), but I couldn't seem to find the right path to get there. I was a people-pleaser, so I wanted others to like me and see me as nice. I followed the rules to avoid any criticism. (Hello again, Sweet Perfect Sue.) Belief in those false tales kept me from networking opportunities—similar to the ball at the prince's castle—where I could have used my voice to meet and talk with influential people. Cinderella wanted to be more and took the risk of attending in her magical gown, but she knew inside that she wasn't the princess everyone else saw. She wanted to fit in with the other ball-goers, but didn't believe that she could. Like Cinderella, I didn't believe that I belonged. I always felt as if I were an impostor. When I thought a situation might not go well, I would self-sabotage and run back to my comfort zone before the stroke of midnight. It was easier to avoid conflict and delay conversations. I wouldn't advocate for myself, and put others first instead. I asked for help from my coach (a.k.a. my fairy godmother), and learned that I needed to trust myself and see the gifts I had to offer. She gave me the truth I didn't want to believe. She said, "If I didn't value myself, how could I expect others to find value in me and my contributions?" That was both difficult and powerful for me to hear. Cinderella took her fate into her own hands when she went to the ball to meet Prince Charming; it was time for me to do the same. I had to get out of my own head (filled with the voice of my own evil stepsister, Victoria) and go find the happily-ever-after that I deserved.

How We Were Raised

MANY OF THE OLD STORIES that lived in my head came from what I learned as a child and internalized into adulthood. You would think that new stories would replace childhood ones as you get older, but they don't unless you know they exist. A research study specific to women may help explain why some of these beliefs persist into adulthood.

In 2015, KPMG International published a study on women's leadership. The research participants included three thousand women aged 18-64. One of the main questions asked in the

Chapter 4

survey was focused on lessons participants learned when they were growing up. The results showed that women were given messages as children that have continued to influence the way they behave as adults. Here are a few of the responses to the question, from highest to lowest percentages:

- 86 percent: Be nice to others.
- 86 percent: Be a good student.
- 85 percent: Be respectful to authorities.
- 77 percent: Be helpful.
- 56 percent: Take a stand for what you believe in.
- 44 percent: Be a good leader.
- 34 percent: Share your point of view.[18]

Look at the messages that were internalized by these women when they were very young girls. Girls were rewarded when they were nice, followed the rules, and helped others. Strong leadership and expressing a point of view rated much lower on the scale. That implies that it was encouraged much less. Lessons learned in childhood do not go away; they are the learned behaviors that women continue to experience as adults. This is a small sample, but in my experience these numbers are in line with my behaviors and those of my clients, friends, and former coworkers. Without role models or new information, beliefs that exist within children will stay with them as they become adults. This is important to recognize if you are managing women on your team who may be holding onto these type of messages from their past.

I have seen that the same issues with limiting beliefs and false stories can exist for men, too—they just don't talk about it as much as women do. Men will show you what their beliefs are through their actions and share them verbally once they build trust with you. Keep in mind that many men were—and some still are—raised to be "tough" and not talk about or show their emotions. That is what their parents were taught, and they gave the same messages to their boys. Men live with beliefs that hold them back, too, but there is a lot of ingrained programming to get through to help them see the truth.

All of us were indoctrinated as children in one way or another. When I came into the world, it was expected that I would be a perfect good girl who stayed quietly in the background. Husbands worked outside the home and made the money; women stayed home and raised the kids. What is valued in women and girls, boys and men has shifted over the years, but for many generations, this was how we were taught to think and behave.

To recent generations, the data in the KPMG study above may seem absurd because there are so many opportunities for women now. As of 2020, the US workforce is currently more than 50 percent female.[19] Women are having success and a huge, positive impact on the economy. I had a role model in my mom to help me see that I could work outside the home and raise children at the same time. She helped me learn that it was possible to have the best of both worlds.

What happened in the past can't be changed, but it is helpful to understand the messages women and men have received and internalized. Leaders need to keep this messaging in mind and dig deeper to understand the beliefs of their direct reports, which may shed a light on the correlation between those beliefs and their behaviors and actions.

Chapter 4

Limiting Beliefs

ONE OF MY OLD LIMITING beliefs was that only the senior leaders could sit at the "big table" during a meeting. I would think to myself: *I respect them, and they are higher on the chain of command. I don't belong there because I am not on the executive team.* I believed that thought for such a long time. I sat at the back of the room and didn't participate. I chose to sit back there because of my belief that I wasn't at the right level to sit at the table. I created my own "invisibility" story. I kept myself from opportunities and hid behind those who chose to be out in front.

Self-limiting beliefs are assumptions or perceptions that can prevent you from going after what you wish to achieve in your life. Here are some examples:

- I am not qualified to do this.
- If I try this, I could fail.
- People will judge me.
- I don't have enough experience.
- I can't apply for that job because I haven't worked at that level before.
- I don't have every experience on that job description, so I shouldn't apply.
- Everybody else is good at this, but I am not.

Does any of this sound familiar to you? Once upon a time, I said every one of those examples to myself to justify why I couldn't go forward into new opportunities. I went into comparison mode and created a story that other leaders had more skills and higher intelligence than my own. I diminished my own experience and kept myself out of the game of being more visible. I discounted my skills to justify why I wasn't ready for more and blamed other people for my lack of success. I focused on being safe instead of putting myself out there more. At that point, I couldn't see the positives that I could have brought to a role.

Byron Katie says, "A thought is harmless unless we believe it."[20] If we look at our thoughts as just thoughts and don't assign any significance to them, they can't hurt us. If you could look at the self-defeating messages in your head and know that they aren't true for you, what might you do instead? What if you chose to believe something different? What if the limiting belief statements from above were reframed to demonstrate a positive, more confident view of who you are? Here are some positive belief statements:

- I am a quick learner, and I will figure out what I don't know.
- I am ready to learn new skills.
- I am excited to try this and be successful at it.
- I know that I can ask for help if I need it.
- I am smart and I have great experience for this role.
- I know I can perform well in this role and take on this new responsibility.
- I don't have all of the required experiences, but I am confident that I can do well in this role.

Your Thoughts

THOUSANDS OF THOUGHTS GO THROUGH your head each day, comprised of stories, beliefs, experiences, ideas, and facts.

Chapter 4

Your thoughts have been influenced by what you learned and experienced as you grew up. Thoughts can be either positive or negative. If you don't monitor or question the thoughts that go through your mind, then you will automatically believe them. I compare it to a movie that you watch on repeat. That "movie" you watch each day becomes the lens through which you see reality and make decisions. Your brain looks at new things to find patterns of information and puts them together with your existing beliefs to confirm that they fit. This is called confirmation bias, and it means you will always be on the lookout for new facts to confirm that the information that you see in your "movie" is the truth.

From Byron Katie's website:[21] "…we remain alert to our stressful thoughts—the ones that cause all the anger, sadness, and frustration in our world—but we question them, and through that questioning the thoughts lose their power over us."

People operate on automatic pilot every single day. Your thoughts drive your behavior, actions, and how others see you. Most people have no idea that the thoughts in their heads are not necessarily reality. Did you know that you have a choice to question your thoughts before you believe them? (I never thought that was an option. It sounds a bit crazy, but it is true.) Decisions are made based on what you think and believe, and thoughts and beliefs may be what hold you back from bigger achievements.

Let me share a situation that I went through to illustrate this point for you. My manager, Melissa, and I were in a session at a technology conference to hear someone speak about the new software we had chosen to implement at our company. We were under a highly aggressive timeline to implement this tool and had started to configure, build out the software, and load data a few months before. Our assumption was that we had a lot to learn from the other people at the conference, whom we believed were further down the path than we were. As we listened to this speaker, who was deemed a customer "expert" on the software, we both realized that we knew way more than we'd thought and could progress much faster. We weren't behind the rest of the pack, we were the leaders!

Melissa turned to me and said, "I have a great idea. We are going to be one of the first companies to implement this software with this level of complexity. You should speak at this conference next year and share our successes with all of these attendees." *Wait, I was with her until she said I should speak here at this conference.* I felt a wave of panic come over me. *I think she said she wanted me to be a speaker at this huge conference.* I knew a lot, but would people think I am some expert to listen to in a session? The thought of a speech in front of a crowd made me anxious. I avoided such situations like the plague.

I went from confidence to doubt in a matter of seconds. My own personal documentary of bad speeches started to play on repeat in my head. I couldn't pay attention to what the presenter said anymore. I told myself to calm down. A year was a long time from now—maybe Melissa would forget this idea by then. (I know, I know, not my finest moment.)

I knew in my heart that I needed to make this speech. I had spoken to her earlier that day about how I could position myself to get a promotion, and this was a step toward that outcome. The truth was that I was scared I might embarrass myself, my boss, and the company. I couldn't say that out loud to anyone, though. The only barrier that would hold me back

Chapter 4

from delivering the speech was me and my old companion, fear. I couldn't let situations that happened long ago keep me from great opportunities right now.

Fast-forward to a year later. I chose to trust myself and speak at the conference. My manager, who had sat by my side one year before, now sat in the front row to cheer me on along with other members of our team. We had created this moment together. I felt a big responsibility to my team to shine a light on what we had accomplished as a group. We were rock stars at this moment. I had to hand it to my boss—she knew a year ago that this was a big chance to seize the spotlight for the work we were about to do. As I stood there, I saw that we had come full circle from an idea that scared me to death to me onstage, speaking in front of all of these people. It went better than I ever could have expected. Once it was over, a line of people formed who wanted to talk to me, congratulate us, and ask me and our team a bunch of questions. I realized in that moment that the scoreboard read Sue—1, Fear—0. Fear did not win that day.

That experience boosted my confidence and helped me learn a big lesson. I could take Old Safety Boulevard or choose New Adventure Way instead. It was time to step onto the bold path to focus on the adventures and experiences that would help me grow into the leader that I knew I wanted to be deep down inside. I will admit that when I am about to do something new, I still have to challenge myself to take New Adventure Way. I make the choice to block out the fear, trust that I can do it, and have confidence in myself. I push myself to choose the bold path each day, and I invite you to come travel along with me. Don't let fear take you on a detour back to safety. Stay on the road that takes you to the places that will help you achieve your potential.

The Invisible Challenge of Visibility

I am so grateful that Kathy (my mentor from Chapter 1) told me what I needed to hear way back when. It forced me into action and set me on this path of learning about myself. Although her feedback was painful to hear at the time, it forced me to take a deeper look at my beliefs, what I wanted, and the actions I could take to get what I wanted. It helped me to diminish the power that those thoughts had over me. We all have incredible value to bring to our personal and professional lives. You are too important to hide at the back of the room and be invisible. If you can learn from my mistakes and take the bolder path, it could change your life.

Visibility Backlash

I WOULD BE REMISS IF I didn't include a section here on what can happen in certain work cultures when women or other underrepresented leaders face challenges if they are assertive or too visible. If the culture is not supportive of these leaders, it creates a difficult work environment in which to succeed and they will choose invisibility instead (or leave the company). They tried to fight the battle without success and now they are disengaged. Would they have been praised if they fell into a different category? This is an important question that all leaders need to ask themselves: Am I an inclusive or exclusive leader?

I see insecure senior leaders who struggle with strong direct reports who could be great complements to them but are instead pushed down, embarrassed publicly, or diminished because the insecure senior leaders see them as a threat. This happens far too often—and then good people who love their jobs leave to go somewhere else. They also face mental and

Chapter 4

emotional distress that has a huge impact on their lives and their careers. The culture in a company needs to be open to supporting everyone's success. The idea that only certain people can be competent leaders is ridiculous. Someone's gender identity, race, age, sexual orientation, religion, or disability does not impact their capacity to be a leader or to do a great job. Let's highlight the fantastic results that the people in the organization get, not diminish their accomplishments.

You will see an approach in the RISE process that leverages partnerships in which people support each other's achievements. This is a good strategy to help women leaders, and leaders from other underrepresented groups shine. "Despite Progress, Gender Gap in Leadership Persists" an article by Matthew Riddle, shared details of a 2018 study by the University of Buffalo School of Management. The study, led by Katie Badura and Emily Grijalva, found that only 26 percent of women held executive roles and men were more often viewed as leaders. This research included over nineteen thousand leaders and compiled over fifty-nine years of data. "This study found that men are more likely to speak up in meetings. The men were louder and more confident during group discussions, but lacked the ability to support their followers' development and success." They gave an example of how women found a way to combat this type of situation: "'In the Obama White House, female staffers adopted a strategy of amplifying one another's comments during meetings and giving credit to the individual who said it first, to ensure that women's voices were being heard,' Badura says. 'Tactics like this help the most qualified individuals stand out and emerge into leadership roles—regardless of gender.'"[22] This approach could also be used to help anyone who is quieter or hesitant to speak in meetings or group conversations.

The Invisible Challenge of Visibility

I have been in male-dominated organizations for my whole career. The changes in culture have been slow, but most companies are now more open to all leaders regardless of gender. The unconscious bias and stereotypes are still there, but we can work together to call them out. When I first started out on this path, it was easier for me to speak out on behalf of my team than for myself. They hadn't yet had the experiences to make them feel confident in these larger group meetings. I wanted them to see that they could do it. I gave them consistent opportunities to be present at the table, and highlighted their accomplishments when they weren't there.

It is also true that employees may have more of a challenge when they have children. Help them readjust as they come back to work from maternity or paternity leave. They may also need additional support when their kids are young. Kids get sick and need to visit the doctor. Find ways to be flexible with employees' work hours to accommodate medical appointments and other family needs. When my kids were younger, I worked at night to make up the time. No number of hours I took off from work to take a child to the doctor could come close to the nighttime hours I put in.

Incorrect assumptions are also made that women with young children aren't interested in career advancement. Women comprise over 50 percent of the workforce. We need to encourage them and continue to give them opportunities to receive high-exposure assignments. Unless they say "I can't do more" or "I don't plan to return to work," ask them what their career goals are. I worked through three pregnancies and returned to high-exposure assignments after each maternity leave. I was very clear that I would return and wanted to continue to advance my career. If you aren't clear with your management, they may make wrong assumptions and you will be stuck. This is an opportunity to use your voice and share what you want.

Gender Assumptions in Leadership

THERE ARE LEADERSHIP CHARACTERISTICS THAT have traditionally been attributed to certain genders, but I am happy to see the lines blur more often now and traits such as empathy, emotional intelligence, and self-awareness are now recognized as the top leadership characteristics that all genders can leverage.

In the research highlighted just a little earlier in this chapter, Badura and Grijalva "attribute the gender gap to societal pressures that contribute to gender differences in personality traits. For example, men tend to be more assertive and dominant, whereas women tend to be more communal, cooperative, and nurturing. As a result, men are more likely to participate and voice their opinions during group discussions and be perceived by others as leaderlike."[23] This is the reason that you need to trust yourself and speak with confidence. You know more than you give yourself credit for, and your management needs to hear from you. Don't hide behind someone else and assume that they know more or are smarter than you. This is your time to share your value with others.

Are You Ready?

IN THE NEXT CHAPTER, WE will start to go through the RISE process so you can build out your visibility plan. The process is simple and easy to follow. However, it may still create some anxiety for you as you look at potential actions to take. Remember that when you step into new actions, it will feel different, but that is what it takes to change the way that people see you. The resistance that you feel is normal. I have been there and know that anything new brings out vulnerability.

We have to rewire old habits, and that can take time. Your ego is a strong critic, and it gives you all kinds of reasons why you can't get out there in front of people. It will tell you to avoid the limelight at all costs because it seems so much easier and less risky. However, you will have a plan that helps keep you headed in the right direction when obstacles arise.

What you are about to learn in the next chapter is the result of my own visibility journey. I would not be where I am today if I had not learned how to create opportunities to show my value; I can say that with complete certainty. I ask for you to be open to the process for yourself and trust it. Don't prejudge whatever comes along; if you can make a difference by your involvement with it, then it could do great things for your career.

You will face unexpected challenges. I want you to be kind to yourself, recognize when you do well, and forgive yourself when you could do better. Focus on the positive and it will change your outlook. Self-acceptance and patience with yourself are so important in these moments. That sounds simple, but it is so important to help you move past all the negativity, criticism, and judgment that may come from you more than anyone else. You are perfect just the way you are. You are worth it—call it out for yourself.

Chapter 4

Actions

1. Capture answers to the following questions in your notes page or notebook. Have you done anything to sabotage or diminish yourself? What could you do to shift your thoughts away from the behaviors that minimize your value? (Here are a couple suggestions: You could call one of your supporters to help you get back on track with your plan, or come to the Be Bold, Be Visible, Be the Leader You Were Meant to Be Facebook group[24] to get support and connect with other leaders who are raising their visibility, too!

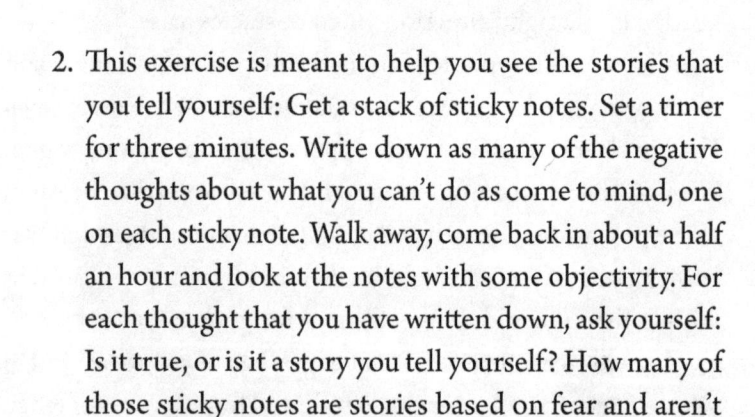

2. This exercise is meant to help you see the stories that you tell yourself: Get a stack of sticky notes. Set a timer for three minutes. Write down as many of the negative thoughts about what you can't do as come to mind, one on each sticky note. Walk away, come back in about a half an hour and look at the notes with some objectivity. For each thought that you have written down, ask yourself: Is it true, or is it a story you tell yourself? How many of those sticky notes are stories based on fear and aren't true? What do you want the story to be instead?

    (An example of one of my own limiting beliefs: *I can't run a half marathon*. I could have stayed with that story, but instead I changed it to *I haven't run a half marathon yet*. I figured out how to train, asked for help from people who have done it and ran the race.)

Notes

is it really a big deal - no turn myself outgit.

- Sabotage - tell myself other people aren't interested in my team/results/me.
- excuse - build + layer sometimes
- not perfect, still room to go —
  share
  not yet

Shift away from this →

FB group.
connect w/ over visible leaders —
people want to raise visibility

RISE STEP ONE: REFLECT

Chapter 5:
DON'T GIVE IN, RISE UP!

"Management doesn't know who you are, and they won't promote someone if they don't know what you can do. I know you have experience, but they need to see you demonstrate your leadership in a bigger way. You will need to figure out the best actions to take to push yourself out of your comfort zone so they can see you."

Nicole left the meeting with her boss more frustrated than ever. She had no idea how to be in front of her management more than she was already. In her mind, she had done more to use her voice in the past few years than she had at both companies she worked at previously combined. As an introvert, she wanted to avoid a lot of attention and had blamed her lack of progress in the past on her management because she thought they played favorites. Now she realized that she had to look in the mirror and own her role in the situation. Nicole knew that a change was needed to allow her to progress in her career.

Nicole was thirty-two years old, married, and had two kids. We met through a friend at a group dinner we attended about five years ago. We sat next to each other and she shared her experience and background during our conversation. Her previous companies were both start-ups, and she had risen to manager level in both of those companies. The pace of the start-ups was relentless. She was involved in all areas of the business and learned so much. However, she didn't take much vacation time and started to burn out. She decided to seek out a bigger company structure with more advancement potential. The supply chain role that she had recently accepted in this three-billion-dollar company excited her so much. It offered an experience for her in the consumer goods industry, and that was new for her. She lit up when she talked about the company. She said, "I feel like I've reached 'the big time'!"

After the conversation with her manager, she remembered that I was a coach and reached out to me to discuss her situation. She gave a few details over the phone about why she wanted to connect with me, and we agreed to meet at her office at the end of the week.

When we met, I asked Nicole to give me some background on what had happened since she joined the company. She responded in a dejected monotone, "I am a senior manager in supply chain. I came into the organization with four years of experience, and I have worked for my current manager for about six months." Nicole was no longer the same person from the dinner who talked about her job in a positive way; now she was negative, frustrated, and nervous to talk about the conversation with her manager. I asked her to share her manager's feedback to see how I could help her, and she relayed it. Then I asked her to describe what the challenge was for her. She said, "I like to get results, and this company has a much slower pace than what I am used to. There are thousands of employees, and that brings a lot more politics and bureaucracy. I have to leverage more resources to get what I need done and that takes more time." As she continued, she rolled her eyes and used her fingers to show me the air quotes as she described the company's "unwritten rules." Then she pulled a notebook from her briefcase to show me her to-do list. It filled the page. She said, "How am I supposed to get all this work done when all I do is sit in meetings all day long? I thought it would be better here."

She rose from her chair and began to pace back and forth. "Also, I don't have a clue why the experience that I have doesn't seem to count unless I demonstrate it here for my current management. It was good enough to get me hired, but now it isn't enough to help me get promoted. It makes no sense." She slumped back down into the chair and leaned on the table with her forehead in her hands. Her body language showed someone who was out of energy and exhausted. She said, "I feel like I make a little progress as I head up the hill, but no matter how long I climb, some obstacle appears to knock me back and I have to start at the bottom again. I don't feel that it is possible for me to get to the top. The motivation and excitement that I felt when I first joined the company is gone, and now it feels like I made a huge mistake. After five years, I feel stuck and unsure if I should stay at the company or leave. I knew that it was time to ask for help or I would continue to stay stuck."

Nicole shared that she wanted me to help her to move to a director role. Based on what she heard from her manager, she knew that she would have to prove she was ready. She still thought it was possible to stay at the company and have success if she could change how she was perceived. She said, "I never had to be strategic in what I did and said. I just came in and did my job. It worked well until now. I have to do something different if I want them to see that I am ready to be a director." As I listened to her, I thought about a process that I had created for clients and wondered if it might work well for her. I shared some of the details and explained that I had used this approach with clients one-on-one, but had now modified it to be a self-driven process. The goal was for my clients to walk through the process and create an action plan for themselves, while I would be there to support them if needed. It was important for them to own the plan since they had to execute it, and it helped create that ownership when they built it themselves.

I had named the process RISE. The acronym stands for reflect, ideate, select, and evaluate. Each client walks through the four steps needed to create their own visibility action plan. Once I finished the explanation, I asked Nicole if she was open to using the RISE process to create her own plan. I told her I would be there to help her but wanted her to try it on her own first. She said, "Yes, that sounds great! How soon can we get started?" Her whole face lit up with excitement as we talked about next steps. I told her I wanted to feature her as a case study in my book that I planned to publish in the next year. She agreed to let me share her responses in the book so that other people could have an example to look at as they created their own plan.

Leadership Success Scorecard

Before we got into the RISE process, I asked Nicole to think strategically about the outcome she wanted. She said, "I'm not sure what you mean." I explained, "In order for your plan to be successful, you will need to demonstrate the leadership traits of a director while you are still in your current role. You want them to see that you already act as if you were a director."

I shared a method for being strategic in what we'd include in the RISE process. I call this the Leadership Success Scorecard approach. It is a simplified version of what I do, but I knew it would work well to get her to focus. I asked her, "What are some of the traits you think of when you observe a director who performs well? If you need ideas for traits to consider, think about someone you respect and what makes them successful. What do you admire about their leadership?" She said, "Okay, I see what you mean. I would choose these traits: confident, strategic, sets a vision, inspires others, challenges the status quo, leads transformational change, and a great communicator." I followed with, "Great, are those the traits that you want to be identified with, too?" She nodded her head yes. "Do you have any others?" She smiled and said, "No, those traits are great. That is how I want to be described by others and how I want to see myself in action each day."

For each trait, I asked Nicole to rate herself on a scale from 1 to 10. Here are her responses:

Leadership Trait	Rating from 1-10 (1 is low and 10 is high)
Confident	4
Strategic	5
Sets a Vision	6
Inspires Others	8

Challenges the Status Quo	5
Leads Transformational Change	4
Strong Communicator	6

I asked Nicole to think about these traits as she designed her action plan. The goal was to focus on actions that would demonstrate the traits that were already strong for her and improve upon those that were lower on the scale.

What traits are important for you to show others in your current role or aspirational roles? Think about the traits that you want others to see in you and your leadership and rate yourself. We will revisit this scale in the last step of the RISE process in Chapter 9 to gauge your progress.

RISE Process — Step One: Reflect

WE DECIDED TO KICK OFF step one of the RISE process, "reflect," right away. Although Nicole was excited to get started, I noticed that as I explained what we would do in this step, she began to shift around in her chair. She looked at her watch a few times and doodled in her notebook. She crossed her arms and looked like she was ready for battle. Her body language spoke loud and clear: *Can't I just go do stuff? I don't know what I would reflect on anyway.* I had seen this type of resistance in other clients, too. It is hard for those who want to get a lot done to slow down and be vulnerable, which is uncomfortable for them. I shared my observation with her. Sure enough, she responded, "Can't we just get to the part where I pick out some new actions to implement?" I explained that this first step is the most important part of the process, and that while it might feel unnecessary and uncomfortable for her, it was actually key to helping her understand the major motivators that would make her promotion goal achievable.

If you don't understand the "why" behind what you do and your desired ultimate outcome, then how will you know if the actions that you take are the right ones, or if they will get you to the right place?

I knew that unpacking in this way was a very different experience for Nicole. I said, "I can tell you how to be visible, but you need to understand why you want it and what you want to get out of it. The time you spend up front will help you gain clarity on the path that you want to take. All the insights that you identify in step one will help you create a better plan and provide motivation for you throughout your journey."

I could see that this journey was a scary one for Nicole, because she had stayed in the background for quite a while and, although she was a manager, she was still a novice when it came to cultivating a leadership presence with her management. She was ready for the next big step and had the capacity to do it. However, she was a self-proclaimed perfectionist and scared to fail or look bad in front of others. She didn't see how good she was, and that held her back from new opportunities. This meant we would focus on ways to demonstrate her confidence and value, but also coach her on how she sees herself. We would work on her confidence and self-trust so that she would be ready for a new opportunity when a position became available.

As I shared with Nicole, when I coach someone, I ask them the questions in the next section in order to help them understand how they think about their situation. Most leaders are doers and don't want to spend the time to think and plan, though I would advocate for them to spend half their time in action and half their time in creating strategy and plans. If a leader doesn't think about their future and that of their team, then who will?

I built the following reflection process so that it can be completed on your own. To move to a higher level or take on more responsibility means you must think bigger and be more strategic. Don't worry about the "how" right now, only focus on what you want to accomplish. Is it big enough to make you uncomfortable? If you want to grow, it can't be a goal that is easy for you.

As we got started on the questions, I gave Nicole a little more context. This reflection time creates the foundation that will help you build out your plan. Remember, these questions are designed to help you think about where you are, why you want visibility, and what outcome you want it to help you create. It is an opportunity to be intentional in your plan from the beginning.

As examples for you, here are my questions and Nicole's responses, below.

The Why Questions: What Motivates You to Raise Your Visibility?

Me: Why do you want visibility?
Nicole: "My manager wants to promote me at some point, but he says the decision makers on our leadership team don't know who I am. I do a good job, but they need to see that I can be a visible leader and that I have the capabilities to do what is needed at the next level. As I reflect on his feedback, I know he is right, but I am not sure how to get in front of the right people and say what is appropriate. This is all new to me."

Don't Give In, Rise Up!

Me: Why is it important for you at this time in your career?
Nicole: "I have been at the company for five years and in my current role for three years. I have taken on project leadership roles and done well with them, but I want to manage a larger team now and take on more responsibility. I need to show management what I can do."

Me: Why do you think others feel that you need visibility?
Nicole: "My manager said that the decision makers don't know me, and that is a disappointment for me to hear. I should schedule time to meet with them and present at meetings so they can hear from me. I confess that I am a bit of an introvert, so it isn't my normal approach to be in front of people at the senior level. I do a good job, but I continue to let other people speak out in meetings while I sit in the back."

The What Questions: What Outcome Do You Want?

Me: What will visibility bring to you?
Nicole: "It will allow the decision makers on my leadership team to know who I am and what I can do. I thought that my hard work was enough, but I can see that if I don't show people what I can do, they will never know. It will also help me to be more confident in front of other people. I hesitate to share ideas or make recommendations in front of a big group. It reminds me of when I was in grade school and didn't want to raise my hand in class. If I can be more visible, it will help me to do that and not hold myself back."

Chapter 5

[margin note: don't like spotlight on me]

Me: What holds you back from visibility?
Nicole: "I think it is my fear of failure. I don't want to embarrass myself in front of a group, especially people who are on my leadership team. I am not like the extroverts in the room who talk a lot and have no trouble with it. I want to plan out what I say so it is perfect, and then I miss my opportunity. I don't want to brag or just talk to talk. Too many people in my organization do that, and people make fun of them. It has been easier for me to stay at the back of the room, but that hurts my chances for success."

[margin note: I can set strategy, drive change, lead team, drive programs]

Me: What do you want other people to see that you can do?
Nicole: "I want them to see that I can make decisions, share recommendations, have confidence to present new ideas, lead a team, and deliver big programs for our company."

Me: What if you don't make any changes and do what you have always done?
Nicole: "I guess I will stay right where I am and not go anywhere. That isn't what I want, and I need to show management that I can be a visible leader."

The How Questions: How Will You Raise Your Visibility?

[margin note: Own run boss present in different forums]

Me: How will you evaluate your success with your visibility plan?
Nicole: "If I start to get good feedback from my manager that he sees a difference in me, I'll know that it is successful."

[margin note: More calls with our team – more requests]

Don't Give In, Rise Up!

Me: How will you stay motivated if what you try doesn't work well?
Nicole: "I know that I can be hard on myself, so that is good for me to think about. I will talk to you about it as my coach and ask some of my peers I trust for help to keep me motivated."

Me: How will you gather feedback from others?
Nicole: "I will share my visibility plan and ask my manager for feedback when we meet one-on-one. I will also ask my clients for feedback when we meet. My manager usually surveys my peers, direct reports, and clients before my midyear and year-end performance reviews, so I can get feedback that way also."

Me: How do others promote themselves?
Nicole: "I see people speak in meetings and promote themselves or their teams. They also stop by regularly to talk with our senior leadership team members; I see them since I sit near senior leadership in the office. I know others who do status reports on a regular basis to share what they accomplished. Until I got this feedback, I saw these additional actions as extra work and I just wanted to do my job. I worried about being someone who brags about everything and sucks up to the boss."

Me: How can you apply what others do to your own visibility strategy?
Nicole: "I could start to do status reports, that isn't too hard. I could use some of these other ideas, too, but I will need to prepare what to say to senior leaders."

Chapter 5

The Who Questions: Who Do You Need Help From?

Me: Who are the important stakeholders who need to see your visibility?
Nicole: "My manager, my leadership team, my peers, and my clients." VP HR, Ex LT.

Me: Who can give you feedback on your progress and results?
Nicole: "My manager, and I can ask other stakeholders to give me feedback, too."

Me: With whom could you work out a visibility partnership? (This is where you help to promote what a partner works on and they do the same for you.)
Nicole: "I have some peers who do great things. I think that we could support each other and promote our projects in front of our leadership team when it makes sense."

Note: If you are at a higher level in a company (i.e., director or VP), you'll find reflection examples from client leaders at those levels in the appendix.

Review

NICOLE AND I SPENT SOME time talking after she finished her responses to the questions. I asked her to go through them with me and discuss how she felt about the process so far. As she reviewed her answers, she said that she felt anxiety and stress. Although she wanted to put herself in front of management, this was her first time at a bigger company and she didn't want to make a fool of herself. I asked her to think about the experiences that she had at her previous companies. "There may be more people here at this company," I said, "but they are just humans. Don't put them on a pedestal. If you can see yourself as an equal, then the fear won't take over your brain—you can think clearly and be calm." I had her take some deep breaths to put her in a calmer place. I assured her that she could do this, and that it just takes practice. "Remember that what you have to say is important and they need to hear it," I reminded her.

We agreed that Nicole would list her short-term goals for the next ninety days and the next six to twelve months. Here are her responses:

Ninety-day Visibility Goals:

- Complete my visibility action plan.
- Share it with my manager.
- Select three actions to begin to implement.
- Gather feedback on progress during one-on-ones with key stakeholders and management.
- Review what works and make changes if necessary.

Six- to Twelve-month Visibility Goals:

- Implement daily actions with consistency, create a new brand, build credibility, and demonstrate readiness for a promotion.
- Gain confidence and take steps toward building relationships with the executive team, so they know who I am.

Chapter 5

> • Share regular updates with my manager and others and ask for feedback on my progress.

I asked Nicole to capture her outcomes during these two periods. Then I said, "Are you ready to come out of the shadows?" She answered, "YES!! Let's go on to step two!"

Actions

1. Record your own responses to the why, what, how, and who reflection questions in step one. Please do that before you proceed to the next chapter.

2. It can be helpful to break down your plan into what you want to accomplish in the short-term and the long-term. Capture your goals for the next ninety days and six to twelve months in your notebook.

    - Ninety-day Visibility Goals
    - Six- to Twelve-month Visibility Goals

*In case you need some inspiration to use when listing your goals, check out this list of goals met—some of the high-level outcomes clients have experienced when they successfully leveraged their visibility plans. (You will need to expand to add more details that include your specific situation and how you will measure success, as Nicole did.) Just make sure you choose goals that challenge you. We want you to stretch a bit.

- Know more and be known by others
- Lead a project/program
- Create perception/a brand
- Influence and sell ideas
- Demonstrate value
- Drive change
- Demonstrate courage
- Build trust
- Build credibility
- Live my own values
- Set a vision
- Be "connected" in the organization
- Motivate others
- Build a stronger network
- Stop playing small
- Gain confidence
- Demonstrate readiness to move to a higher (or different) role
- Lead and develop my team
- Create external visibility
- Be viewed as a thought leader
- Increase responsibility and scale leadership
- Demonstrate strategic thinking
- Expand my executive presence

Notes

RISE STEP TWO: IDEATE

Chapter 6:
THAT'S A GREAT IDEA!

Nicole had reflected on what she wanted her management to see in her and how the actions she took could help her. Now that she had that information, we began to talk about the ideas and actions that she wanted to implement. To give her context, I shared that this, step two in the RISE process, is focused on creating a list of ideas for action that aligned with the goals that she identified for herself in step one. I said to her, "The intention is to select actions that are strategic and purposeful, aligned with your goals, so that you get the biggest return on your time and effort."

Nicole said, "I am not sure where to begin with this step." I told her that that it is very common, and we would walk through it together.

I asked Nicole if she had any ideas that she wanted to add to her plan, and explained that the goal was to be open to any ideas at this point and not to discount any idea as a possibility.

For now, just write down all of your ideas. You can decide which of them to include when you go through step three, the selection process, in the next chapter. Noting an idea doesn't mean that you must do it; it is just good to record all of them so you don't forget them. I gave Nicole a list of questions to help her capture ideas. I have listed them for you below, along with Nicole's responses.

Let's Come Up with Ideas

Me: What have you seen other people do to gain visibility?
Nicole:
- "I have seen other people talk so much in the room and say nothing."
- "Build upon someone else's response in a meeting or ask a question that is similar but slightly different from one that has already been asked."
- "Make presentations to senior management."

Me: What have you seen other people do that you don't want to imitate?
Nicole: "I don't want to be a braggart. I also don't want to be someone who sends status reports but never gets results."

Me: What do you do outside the office that could be defined as visible?
Nicole: "I lead the food bank volunteer group for my church. I also lead the board at my daughter's school."

Me: What is the craziest visibility idea that you have? (Yes—the craziest!)

Chapter 6

Nicole: "I can't think about doing either of these, but the craziest couple of ideas that I can come up with are to speak at a conference and to do a TED Talk."

Me: What do you do now to be visible, but could take to the next level?
Nicole:
- "I thought that I gave my team visibility, but I can see that there is so much more that I can do for them."
- "I meet with people who are on my project team, but I haven't managed up enough."

Me: What ideas did you come up with that you want to include in your plan? Capture them in your notebook.
Nicole:
- "Give my team more opportunities to be visible and talk about the things that they do."
- "Meet with senior management, not just the people who are on the project team."

It is great to come up with your own ideas for your plan. For some people, it is more challenging to identify ideas. For these clients, I created a list of ideas to use as thought starters. It has helped them to have some additional ideas to review and see if they might apply in their own visibility plans.

The categories below will help you see the different areas in which visibility actions can be accomplished. If you have strengths in certain areas, then you may want to consider one of those categories first when you get to the selection process in chapter 8. There are twelve different categories to select from, so you could start with an area that you are familiar with before you move into other options. Here are the twelve categories:

- Management
- Meetings
- Communication
- Promoting others
- Leading
- Volunteer
- Mentor/Sponsor
- Networking
- Speaking
- Teaching/training
- Social media
- Writing

The Visibility List

OFTEN, WHEN CLIENTS COME TO work with me, they aren't sure where to start. Raising their visibility feels big, and they don't want to fail. That is normal. Many of them are overachievers and want to do well. And of course I wouldn't expect them to have all the answers—they haven't done this before! When I ask them what they think they should do, they identify actions that they see others taking. They don't have any other frame of reference, so once they learn more about what they can do, they get excited. What I coach them on are the small, consistent actions they can take every day that will change how they are viewed.

Chapter 6

I started to capture ideas in a notebook to share with clients and, as the list grew, I moved it to a Word document. To give them inspiration, I have shared this list countless times with people who want to work on ways to stand out. Over time, the list has continued to grow! Most people look at the list and see visibility actions that are so much easier than they imagined. They may do some of these things already, but without consistency. Consistency and intention are key for success. You want people to notice your new behaviors, but not assume that they are a fluke or something you did one time.

You will see many ideas to choose from on the list below, but please don't let that make you feel overwhelmed. I didn't want to leave any ideas off the list that might be helpful for you. Just take your time to review it at your own pace. There is no rush.

The list below is organized into the three levels that you learned about in the Introduction and Chapter 1. To review, here are the descriptions for each level:

- **Getting Started**—Have minimal experience with and focus on visibility.
- **Some Experience**—Have tried to do some things to stand out, but want to do more and improve skills.
- **Experienced**—Have visibility, but want to do more to expand higher-level influence.

Trust how you feel as you read through the list and capture the ideas that interest you. Here are some things to consider as you read through the list:

That's a Great Idea!

1. These actions can be performed in person or in a remote work environment. Working in a remote environment doesn't mean that you can't be visible, but you may have to get creative as to how you do it. You may have to think outside of the box to accomplish some of these actions.

2. These ideas are not duplicated in the different levels. Though you may be at a higher level in the organization, look at where you are from a visibility standpoint. My recommendation is to begin with the "getting started" level and proceed from there. If you feel as if you have already tried many of the ideas at that level, then you can head to the next level! If you have a team or you mentor someone, you may get a new idea from the getting started level of the list to share with them.

3. We will select ideas in step three, the next step in the RISE process. For now, read through the list and look for the ideas and actions that seem authentic to you. Take your time and consider whether these ideas align with the goals that you set for yourself in the previous chapter.

4. Pull out your notebook and write down any of the below ideas that interest you to go along with the list of ideas that you came up with earlier in this chapter.

Chapter 6

LEVEL: GETTING STARTED

Management

Spend Time with Your Manager

- Schedule regular one-on-ones with your manager to share updates with them.
- Ask for feedback on a regular basis and share your development goals.
- Ensure that your manager knows what you want to do in your career. Managers are the ones included in the conversations about future roles, and they need to know your career interests. You need to know if you have their support or if there are other areas that you need to work on to get their support before a role becomes available.

When You Get a New Manager

- Take the initiative to schedule a one-on-one to introduce yourself.
- Get to know them. Ask questions to learn about their management style, their priorities, and details about their personal life if they want to share. Look for connection points that you have in common. The goal is for you to understand how best to work with them.
- Discuss how you will work together and what mode of communication is best (email, text, call).
- Prepare a review of your background, experience, and current responsibilities. Share information about the projects and

programs you lead. Include the status of each and issues, and risks associated with them, where you need management support, etc. Your manager needs to hear this information from you, not from someone else.
- Learn what is important to them and what their vision is for the group. How can you incorporate that information into what you communicate, measure, and manage so that you demonstrate greater support for your manager?

One-on-Ones with Other Key Stakeholders (Internal Networking)

- Meet with key individuals within your own team, group, and client teams and expand your internal network out to other parts of the organization. Look for the decision makers, influencers, connectors, and clients who could have an impact on you, your career, or your projects.
- Schedule skip-level one-on-ones with senior leaders (skip-level means meeting with your manager's manager or executive leadership team). Be your own best advocate: let them get to know you. Share what you have accomplished and about your future career plan.

Meetings

Speak Up in Meetings

- Be sure you sit at the table or at the front of the room. People need to see you as an equal member of the group. There are subtle messages sent and judgments made, and you want to

show that you belong to the group as much as anyone else does. This is also about the elimination of pedestals between levels. You belong at the table, and you can use your voice just as much as anyone else.
- Find an opportunity to make a recommendation or share what you or your team have done.
- Volunteer to share an update on a project that you have done, or sell one of your ideas.
- Be yourself and share your opinions. Do not be afraid to do this. The details you share will help others make good decisions.
- Ask smart questions to show your engagement and be strategic to demonstrate thought leadership in the conversation.

Learn from Others in Meetings

- Observe the people who have the role that you want or who find ways to stand out. What can you learn from them? Can you adapt any of their actions to make them authentic to you?
- What questions do they ask? How do they phrase their questions? Capture the questions that are most effective and modify them so you can ask a question next time.
- Can you see the opportunities that others take to offer help with an issue or problem? How can you do that in your area?
- Do you already know everyone in the meeting? If not, take the opportunity to contact them right after the meeting to introduce yourself in person or over email. Schedule time with them and build new connections. This is a great way to expand your network, and if you do it right away, it will be genuine and sincere.

That's a Great Idea!

Communications

Group Communications

- If your company or group has a newsletter, use it to give an update on a big initiative that you and your team have implemented or are in the process of implementing. This could also be a video that is published on an internal site to teach or share information.
- Share updates on planned volunteer or social activities.
- Send high-exposure status updates to senior leaders and key clients when it makes sense. This gives senior leaders an opportunity to hear from you, and for you to get your name in front of them. You want to make sure that they know who you are and what you do.
- You are onstage whether you realize it or not. Every interaction is an opportunity to share what you have done. Be prepared and intentional and make it count.

Communicate through Conversations

- Share stories that highlight your strengths and accomplishments in a conversational manner. Share details so that people remember you. Be positive, enthusiastic, and make a connection.
- Prepare an "elevator speech" that highlights what you do and who you are in thirty seconds or so. Memorize it and practice it to speak with confidence.
- Use a hallway conversation to work in a win that you have accomplished. In a remote work situation, schedule time with

people for a fifteen- or thirty-minute "virtual hallway" chat. Here are some ideas for what you can mention. Be intentional with what you share about yourself, a team member, or a visibility partner.

- An example of how you influenced an outcome.
- A way in which you drove a key decision.
- An accomplishment you want them to hear about.
- Results or accomplishments of a team member that you want them to hear about.

The Art of the Status Report

- Send a weekly status report to your manager (or other stakeholders) so that you can show what you (and your team) accomplished, decisions you made, recommendations you put forward, where you influenced change, and what you did that demonstrates your leadership.
- Status reports can be effective when your manager is in another location or not as available to you in person.
- When you send status reports consistently, there are a few major benefits:

  - The reports serve as a way for your boss to access information when they need it.
  - You get to manage the perceptions that people have of you and take time to prepare what you want to say.
  - The reports capture what you (and your team) have done and make it easy to create your end-of-year review.

Promoting Others

Create a Visibility Partnership

This is a way to leverage one of your stronger relationships to promote the work that each of you do. Both partners find ways to advocate, in meetings or conversations, for what the other has accomplished. This is very effective, because anytime someone else speaks about what you do, their comments have more weight than they would if you made them yourself.

Leading

Special Project/Event

- Lead or coordinate a big event for your company.
- Volunteer to be on a task force to drive a new process, decision, or recommendation.
- If there is a problem that needs to be solved, volunteer to lead the work to get it fixed. Make sure you talk about what you did and how you did it. Status reports can be used here in an effective way.

Subject Matter Expert (SME)

- Leverage your knowledge and become known as an expert. Go deep into your subject to become the person everyone listens to about it. (Note: You may get stuck in a role if you are the only one who knows everything about a certain subject.

Ensure that you have a backup who knows what you know, so you can move to another role if you have the opportunity.)
- To establish your credibility, create lunch-and-learn opportunities to present information and help others learn what you know. They will automatically see you as an SME.
- Volunteer to lead a class and teach others what you know on an in-depth level.
- Create videos in which you talk about your strengths. This is an opportunity to educate others and create credibility.

What You Do in Your Current Role

- Go above and beyond in your current role to demonstrate that you are ready for the next level. Show that you can do the job before you get the job.
- Find and take opportunities to talk about what you have accomplished in conversation with influencers or management.
- Provide opportunities for your team to get exposure to management in meetings. Introduce what they will present and then let them present the details. This establishes you as the leader and still lets your team shine.

Leverage External Leadership Opportunities

- Take on a leadership role on a school board or nonprofit board, or with a charity or military reserve. These external opportunities can help to establish your credibility at work and create a positive perception that you have leadership capabilities, no matter what role you are in now.

- Lead a networking group, or create an online community that gives you opportunities to speak or share your knowledge in front of a group.

Volunteer

- Take the opportunity to volunteer with task forces, diversity groups, community groups, or conference panels. This can be done either internally, in your company, or externally with groups you are passionate about and can use your leadership.
- Volunteer at your local high school or college to do mock interviews or speak to a class about your career and the lessons that you have learned.

Mentor

- Find a mentor. Ensure that they have credibility and the experience you need, and that you feel that you can have a trusting relationship with them.

Networking

- Attend an external networking event. It is important to have a plan for what you want to accomplish when you attend. If you're able to get information about who will attend, you can get a head start on identifying the people you want to meet.
  - Connect with participants prior to your arrival, if you can, and ask if they want to meet for an introduction and conversation.

Chapter 6

- Learn about everyone you meet—who they are and how you can add value to their lives. This isn't the time to focus only on yourself. This is an opportunity to add value first and to help your new connections remember you. Connect with them on LinkedIn after you leave and invite them to meet with you if you are interested in a longer conversation.
- What outcome do you want to take away from your time at the event, and how can you ensure that you do? You will be able to meet with a lot of people, but for a limited amount of time. You will need to be efficient to achieve your outcome.
- If you are an introvert and these situations are uncomfortable for you, you will need to plan your approach before you get there. One easy trick is to think of yourself as the host. Pretend the event is a party that you are hosting, and you want to make sure people have what they need. You will be surprised how that changes the paradigm for you and makes it easier to approach a group.

Speaking

- Speak to a class of students about a topic you know well.
- Start your own podcast, or be a guest on other people's podcasts.

Teaching/Training

- Teach a class within your company on a topic in which you have expertise.

- Create a webinar or online course on this topic that is open, and would be of interest, to people outside your company.

Social Media

- Comment on, like, and share other people's posts to generate additional followers and connect with the authors of those posts.

Writing

- Post articles on LinkedIn, Medium.com, or other online venues to share what could be helpful for others.

LEVEL: SOME EXPERIENCE

Management

Spend Time with Your Manager

- Ask questions to learn about your manager's vision for the organization. What are their concerns, challenges, and opportunities? How can you support them?
- Make recommendations for organizational changes, process improvements, or cost savings opportunities to show that you are focused on the big picture of company needs.

- Look for opportunities to take the initiative with projects or responsibilities. Become your manager's right-hand person, the one they delegate to and send to meetings on their behalf.
- Become a trusted advisor to your manager so you can learn more about the political landscape of the organization. Ask questions and learn more about what happens in the organization.

When You Get a New Manager

- Share your perspective on your department's vision, strategy, goals, priorities, strengths, opportunities, and risks with your manager. Help them understand what is going well and where you may need their help in the future. If they are new to the company, you may have to give them more context so they can see how your department fits into the company vision. Involve your team, if you can, so they too get exposure to this new leader.
- Become the person who helps the new leader get acclimated to the company faster. This may be through connections you make for them, information you share with them, or insight into the political landscape you can offer. If they aren't successful, it could be detrimental for you. This is your opportunity to add value in a big way.

One-on-Ones with Other Key Stakeholders (Internal Networking)

- Align with people of influence on a regular basis. Understand what their goals are and become familiar with current programs

in their area and updates on their team members. Share the same information from your area. These relationships are critical to getting things done in an organization. They also allow you to take advantage of an informal network in which to learn, sell your ideas, and share information outside of your management structure.
- Pre-meetings may also be necessary to align on ideas and get buy-in from decision makers or influencers prior to a larger discussion. It helps to have allies in the room who have already given you input or offered objections, so you can address them in the discussion. If the conversations don't go well, then you may also need to have a post-meeting with the people who are not on board with your plan.

Meetings

Speak Up in Meetings

- If you are hosting a meeting, make sure that you keep it on track and act as a good facilitator. Give other people an opportunity to speak up. (If you have remote participants, ensure that they can hear and get a chance to speak.)
- If someone talks too much, you may need to interrupt to get your point across. You can say, "That is such a great point; I wonder if you have considered this other option as well?" or "That is great information, thank you for sharing it with the group. Let's take that offline and discuss it tomorrow. We need to circle back to the agenda so we can stay on track with the meeting." This isn't rude, but inserts your voice and establishes your authority to facilitate the conversation and

move it along. It will also increase the respect that people have for you.
- Demonstrate the courage to make big decisions or recommendations. If it is the best thing for the company, you are always right. These are the moments that can define your career, so don't be afraid to take a risk and trust your gut even if you may stand alone.

Learn from Others in Meetings

- Pay attention to the dynamics between the people in the room. Who is an influencer in the room? Who is a decision maker? Who is not aligned with others in the room? What nonverbal communication is happening? All of this information will help you understand who to connect with and various other implications of the dynamic.
- Note any new information from meetings that your team doesn't attend so that they can be informed.
- Can you leverage what you learn in a meeting to your advantage? Identify an impact, process improvement, opportunity, or cost savings that might help you, your team, or another group. This will help you prepare for challenges before they arise and be one of the first to communicate an issue.

Communications

Group Communications

- If you lead a team, department, or organization, it is important for you to meet with your team on a regular basis and establish

consistent opportunities for communication. Your words and actions must match to build trust.
- Be a leader who communicates with strength and integrity. This will create a loyal group of team members who will share information with you and help you push through deadlines.
- When an organizational change occurs, it creates uncertainty. You must be the one to communicate in a calm and composed manner. Leaders who do this will keep their teams calm. Leaders who don't will fight a battle every day to keep the team aligned. Provide transparency where you can to build trust. Without communication from you, the team will create their own stories.

Communicate Through Conversations

- If you are in an office, walk around and check in on your team. Don't just check in on their work, but also on how things are going in their lives outside of work. If you aren't in an office and you work remotely, send an instant message to check in or schedule a quick video call. Ask how things are with your team's kids, families, hobbies, etc. This must be genuine, or they will feel that you are doing it because you think you should, not because you have a real interest in them.
- Consistent one-on-ones are important to ensure engagement, and they allow your team members to get feedback, direction, or guidance to move forward. Leaders who don't make their team a priority will have disengaged team members who leave the company.
- When there is a problem, be proactive and prepare your manager or senior leadership for the impact. Explain the implications and possible solutions so they can decide what

to do or communicate to the next level if needed. This is an opportunity for you to be visible with them and own both the situation and the solution.

The Art of Using the Status Report

- Leverage a status report with key data to help drive resource needs or to highlight an issue that needs to be addressed. (Show the amount of work that your team is handling to demonstrate the need for an additional resource or to push back on work that belongs in another part of the company.)
- Use status reports to position key decisions, issues, and risks. Identify plans for mitigation and solutions for long-term change.

Promoting Others

- When you promote the good that other people do, it helps to strengthen your relationships and credibility and build a larger network of trusted peers.
- If it is too uncomfortable to share what you have done yet, start to advocate for people on your team first. Once you get comfortable, you can find opportunities to do more of this for yourself.

Leading

Leading a Team or Large Project

- Lead or coordinate a program or project that gives you opportunities to update senior management.

That's a Great Idea!

- Attend steering committee or senior management meetings. Present to the leadership team as often as you can.
- Focus on the development of your team and help provide them with opportunities to get in front of management and earn promotions. Members of other teams watch to see which managers develop and support their team members. You will be noticed, and team members will want to work for you.

Special Project/Event

- Vendor negotiations and acquisitions or divestitures are great opportunities to lead with high visibility, if you can be part of the discussions.
- Lead a project to evaluate a new tool or software that the company needs.
- Lead a charity fundraiser or a team-building activity for your group.

Subject Matter Expert (SME)

- Communicate your team's responsibilities clearly so that people who have questions go to them first. Explain to your team that you are an escalation point if needed, but you want to create opportunities to empower your team and let them demonstrate ownership of their responsibilities.
- Governance, policy, and procedure knowledge is more valuable as you move to the next level. You may be the person responsible for such areas because decisions made at this level have higher implications for the organization and bring a lot of exposure.

Chapter 6

Performing in Your Current Role

- When you move to a higher level, you are expected to go above and beyond your current role and take on more responsibilities outside of your day job. This may be an opportunity to lead a task force, reorganization effort, or other high-exposure program. Look for what you can lead that leverages your strengths and gives you the opportunity to show another side of your leadership.
- Look for opportunities to streamline processes, close gaps, identify cost savings, reduce head count, and help the company's bottom line.
- Your role will start to shift from tactical to strategic, and you will need to change your paradigm to think that way. Take the time to focus on your plans and meet with the influencers who can help you drive your goals forward. Strategic initiatives offer more exposure and help you be visible to others, but behind the scenes one-on-one alignment conversations also provide opportunities to show your value.

Volunteer

- Organize a charitable event, or drive an initiative across your organization or team.
- Lead an employee resource group that allows you to work with a sponsor and create a leadership team that works under you and helps you get things done.
- Post pictures online to show that you are a part of the big events hosted by your company.

Mentor/Sponsor

- Become a mentor to junior members of your organization. Mentorship is a great way for you to share your stories of success or failure and lessons learned.
- Leverage senior-level mentors who can help give you guidance and accelerate you to a higher level.
- Volunteer to be a mentor at work, in your community, or through a company like Menttium that creates formal mentoring relationships.
- Identify potential sponsors and build relationships with them. They have to decide if they will sponsor you, but they can advocate for you and help you make real change happen in your career. (Refer back to Chapter 3's section on the mentors and sponsors if you need clarity on which is right for you.)

Networking

- Make an external one-on-one connection, and meet for coffee or lunch and a discussion. This will allow for a longer conversation and for you to learn more about each other.
- Connect with people in discussion groups (i.e., LinkedIn, Facebook, and technical forums) to discuss a challenge you have—and perhaps meet in person.
- Start a community on Facebook or LinkedIn, or a Meetup group, to bring people together around shared interests. People will see you as a thought leader.
  - Meet like-minded people who may be in your industry, share your area of expertise, or are part of a group that

you have an affinity with based on a factor such as gender, religion, political affiliation, or support for a specific cause.

- Connect with people in similar roles at other companies (that are not competitive with your company) to share perspectives and ideas and learn from each other. Look for opportunities to quickly adapt new ideas that show your strategic side and help your management see you in a new way.

Speaking

- Present at conferences about a project or your subject matter expertise.
- Be a part of a panel at a local affinity group meeting or conference.
- Lead a town hall or department meeting. You can be the emcee and facilitate to allow others to speak, plan the events, and provide direction to your organization. This will give you a chance to be in front of your leadership.

Teaching

- Become a part-time teacher at a local college in your area of expertise, or in an area that you are passionate about. Let the students benefit from your experience and establish external credibility.

Social Media

- Post articles on LinkedIn, Medium.com, or other online venues to share what could be helpful for others.

- Create social media posts and articles that build a community of engaged followers.

Writing

- Write about your experiences in a blog or for online magazines, newspapers, or digital sites to establish yourself as a thought leader.
- Write an e-book or a book on a topic for which you are a subject matter expert, and build credibility that way.

LEVEL: EXPERIENCED

Management

Spend Time with Your Manager

- Schedule regular one-on-ones with your manager to talk about program and team progress. Look for opportunities to take on more and learn what is happening that isn't discussed in the open.
- Ask questions when you don't understand a decision or want to make sure it is the right one (even when a decision was made by your manager or someone higher). It will help you learn the background of the situation and shows that you aren't someone who simply takes orders, but rather someone who wants to do the right thing for the company.

Chapter 6

- When organizational shifts occur, come to discussions with recommendations and ideas.
- Take the initiative to handle things before you are asked and drive change in your own organization.
- Discuss strategy and any obstacles that need to be addressed. Share any risks that need to be managed. Talk about communication and where influence is needed to move things ahead.

When You Get a New Manager

- Establish yourself as a smart, respected, strategic, well-connected leader. Report on the status of and contexts for programs, people, and technology. This will help a new leader understand what they've walked into and how you can support their success.
- Align on big programs. You need your manager to understand and support you if there are issues between teams, clients, vendors, etc.
- Discuss any hot topics that could blindside your new manager.

One-on-Ones with Other Key Stakeholders (Internal Networking)

- Politics play a bigger role as you get to senior levels in a company. You have to align with influencers and decision makers to move your agenda forward. Figure out what you can do to stay on key stakeholders' good side and stay one step ahead of the next organizational chess move.
- Prepare for organizational changes before they happen. Is your team large enough that others might target it for

takeover, break it apart, or reduce head count? How can you show others the value of your team so you can minimize impact on the team itself?
- Look for opportunities to share what your team or organization does. Remove obstacles and ensure that the team has what it needs to succeed (funding, resources, alignment).

Meetings

Speak in Meetings

- Prepare and plan for what needs to be accomplished in a meeting.
- Be prepared for what could be discussed in the meeting. You may also need to think on your feet when unexpected topics arise. The ability to handle that pressure, and tough discussions, is vitally necessary.
- Support your team in public to help them get recognition, new roles, and funding for projects, and create a positive perception of them amongst senior management.

Learn from Others in Meetings

- Learn from senior leaders. How do they handle conflict and tough conversations? What questions do they ask of their team and their peers? What would you do if you were in their position?
- Once you know what people are most concerned about, you can prepare options. Watch who aligns and how they handle conversations; you can learn a lot about how to do this yourself.

- Learn about other leaders' chief concerns. Do they care about certain projects, programs, financials, strategies, or individuals? How does this knowledge help you?

Communications

Group Communications

- Leverage group communications to your advantage. Is there a message that everyone needs to hear?
- Leverage group communications to announce organizational changes. This demonstrates that you made or helped to make decisions that led to these changes. It also makes it much easier for everyone to know who to work with and empowers your team to own their roles.
- Create internal marketing communications to help to share what your group or team does. Perceptions are held of groups as well as people. If you need to shift a perception, focus on a visibility plan and communications that help change how others see the group.
- Leverage opportunities to nominate your team or company for external awards that recognize their work. This helps everyone see the great things you have accomplished with your team and your company.

Communicate through Conversations

- Demonstrate consistency between your words and your actions. People will see through you if you don't and lose trust in you.

- The conversations you have keep your finger on the pulse of what happens in the organization. Keep them flowing.
- Have an opinion. Be a thought leader and share your ideas with others. People will look to you for direction.
- Determine who you can and cannot trust. Share information with those that you trust and learn how to read the room. Pay attention to both what is said and to nonverbal communication. This can help you determine who the influencers and decision makers are so you can connect with them.

Promoting Others

- Your team's visibility is very important. Show that you support them publicly so your management can see that they are ready for future roles.
- If one of your team members wants to take another role somewhere else, you must decide if you will support them. Do you want to help them get there? Would your management support the move? If you can't vouch for the person, then why would your management or another group want to work with them? Keep them in front of your management to show your support if you want them to succeed.
- Find ways to praise and uplift women, underrepresented minorities, and introverts who may not fit the profile of someone who is visible. Use your influence to ensure that they are assigned to projects or programs where they can shine. Support them behind the scenes if they need guidance.
- Sponsor an employee resource group to help underrepresented groups in the organization gain new opportunities. Teach

them what you have learned about how to self-promote and talk to other leaders in the company about their accomplishments.

Leading

Leading a Team or Large Project

- Teach your team what you have learned and set the example for them to follow so they can see how it has helped you.
- Prepare your team before meetings so they know what is expected. Have them share what they will present and prepare them for the possible scenarios that might occur. In this way, you will help them learn how to think and prepare on their own.
- It is your role to make sure your team is ready for their opportunities in the spotlight. This holds true for a project team as well.
- You are accountable and responsible for ensuring that progress is on schedule and on budget.
- You also need to be prepared to answer the tough questions or to stand alone when necessary. Do your own homework so you can speak to what you may be asked and prepare for what could happen.

Special Project/Event

- Lead a portion of the work in an acquisition, divestiture, or merger opportunity to drive change, communication, and decisions across the organization. This type of role can be great, but also brings a lot of pressure. You will be in the spotlight and need to be on your game to see a positive result on the scoreboard (to use a sports analogy).

Performing in Your Current Role

- Look for opportunities to streamline processes, identify cost savings, close process gaps, and reduce head count to help the company's bottom line. Help your team get recognition for accomplishments.
- Be strategic: Look at everything (projects, resources, vendors, teams, management) as an opportunity for improvement. You will train your brain to look for impacts, solutions, and ways to remove obstacles.
- What if something went wrong and you were the only leader around to lead it? Would you attend to the problem if it wasn't your responsibility? Step into a crisis to lead the way out, and it will change management's perception of you.

Volunteer

- Build a partnership with a nonprofit or charitable organization. You could help promote them, raise money on their behalf, or connect them with other funding sources or support. This could make a huge difference for the organization and help you gain confidence in your own ability as well.

Mentor/Sponsor

- Become a sponsor for a large program or volunteer organization in your company that needs help and find ways to support

them. These programs or groups may center on women, underrepresented minorities, or employees who are more introverted and need some support to join larger activities.
- Become a mentor or sponsor for individuals you believe have the potential to do well in the organization, but need your credibility to help them succeed.
- If a mentoring program doesn't exist in your company, create one. Start off with a controlled set of mentees and mentors so you can get feedback to make changes if necessary. Once you have established the program, you can expand it to a broader group of participants.

Networking

- Appearances are expected at external networking events. Set the example for others and make introductions for your team with other key influencers.
- Strategically leverage your vendors to learn industry insights and build connections with other companies in your area.
- Schedule time for informational interviews with people you want to learn from so they can get to know you, too.
- It is always important to focus on networking, and it can be done even when you have a great job. It is better to be prepared with a strong network if and when you need it.

Speaking

- Speak at internal and external conferences or panels to represent your company. This puts both you and your company in the spotlight.

Social Media

- Tag other leaders in articles you post to broaden the conversation and build additional opportunities for you to be seen as a thought leader.
- Create a group on a topic that you are passionate about to build a community. Go live, post articles, and add value to the group.

Writing

- Write a book that changes the world. You have a unique set of experiences and ideas that could help someone learn or see a new perspective. Published authors enjoy some built-in credibility; not everyone wants to spend the time required to write and publish a book.

Idea Collection

NICOLE TOOK HER TIME AND went through the list of ideas. She was excited to see that there were so many doable possibilities to choose from! She had not considered some of them before, and as we talked, they seemed less scary than she thought they would be. Is that true for you, too? Sometimes we make something bigger in our heads than it should be, or overcomplicate what needs to be done.

Once Nicole read through the list, I asked her, "What visibility level do you think you are at now?" She answered, "I am at the getting started level." Then I asked her to "share the categories that resonated with you the most." She replied,

Chapter 6

"My choices in the management, meetings, promoting others, mentor, and communication categories are the ones I want to try first."

Which ideas do you want to consider for your plan? Nicole identified the ideas that resonated with her the most and listed them below by category.

Category: Management
- Idea: Schedule time with influencers to ensure that they get to know me better and I can build a relationship with them.
- Idea: Schedule skip-level one-on-ones with my manager's manager and with my manager's peers so they get to know me and I can shift their perception of me.
- Idea: Spend time with my manager and question him to learn more about what happens in the organization.

Category: Promoting Others
- Idea: Implement a visibility partnership with one of my peers.
- Idea: Do more to get my team in front of the right people.

Category: Communications
- Idea: Send my manager a weekly status report of what I have accomplished this week and the plan for the next week.

Category: Mentor
- Idea: Identify a mentor I can meet with and get advice from when I run into challenges.

That's a Great Idea!

Category: Meetings
- Idea: Pre-meetings will help me align with influencers on the ideas I want to get approved. I will also implement post-meetings if there are still questions to be answered.

I asked Nicole if the ideas she captured on the list above felt authentic to her. I explained, "If the ideas don't feel authentic, then they will drain your energy and make you feel like an impostor. Our goal is to help you see how you can do this in a way that allows you to be yourself. Yes, these ideas may push you out of your comfort zone, but they shouldn't feel false." I took her through a validation of what she had captured on her list. Here are the questions that I asked her to complete and her answers.

Validate Your List of Ideas

Me: Look at the key takeaways from your reflection in step one. Do these ideas align with your why?
Nicole: "Yes—I was excited to see how many options there are for me to try. I thought about what my manager said in my feedback session as I went through the list. I like the ideas that I listed, and I believe they will be a great start to help me change how I am perceived."

Me: Can you identify the items that resonated the most with you when you first read through your list?
Nicole: "The ideas that focused on management discussions. My manager said that people don't know who I am, and he is

right. I have not met with his peers or his manager at all. I was focused on the job and not the relationships that I should build."

Me: Are the ideas authentic to you and your style?
Nicole: "Yes, I believe that they are authentic to me, and I can see how to implement them now that I have gone through this exercise. Before I talked to you, I tried to make this process hard, and it is so simple. When you know what will make a difference in helping you accomplish your goal, it doesn't seem that scary, and I know that I can do these things that I wrote down. I know my list will be something I have to focus on every day."

Me: Will the ideas you identified help you achieve your goal?
Nicole: "Yes, I believe that they will."

Me: Do you feel that your list of ideas will push you out of your comfort zone enough to help others see you in a different way?
Nicole: "Yes. The one that is out of my comfort zone is the skip-level meetings. I can see that this is something I should have been doing all along, but I can rectify that now. If I can do this well, it will start to shift things for me."

Me: Will you need help from other people, or can you implement them on your own?
Nicole: "I will share my completed plan with my manager so he can support me as I work on these new actions. I will also identify a visibility partner who can help me and that I can help too."

That's a Great Idea!

Whew! I know that was a lot to go through in this one chapter. I hope the list sparked new ideas that help you see what is possible for you to accomplish! I also hope it helped you see that there is another way, and that you can do this with success. That doesn't mean it will be easy—but you *can* do it.

You have taken the first two steps toward creating a new path for yourself! Congratulations!!

Remember, though, this is a marathon and not a sprint. There is no pressure. Do what feels right for you and go at your own pace, but don't stop. Remember the goals that you laid out for yourself in Chapter 5. Those goals are what I want you to focus on, because the result is what's important, not how fast you get there. Just focus on the results that you want to achieve and stay on the path.

Before we continue, I want to prepare you for something unexpected that you may experience as you go through this process. We've already touched on impostor syndrome, but the next chapter has more detail. It may or may not happen for you, but most high achievers have some form of impostor syndrome. Deep down, we feel that we don't deserve what we want. Does this sound like you or someone on your team? We will take a brief little detour from the RISE process to go through impostor syndrome and its potential impacts in the next chapter. We will get back on track with step three of the RISE process after that. Sound good?

Actions

I DO A CHECK AT the midway point in a coaching session, and we are now at the midway point of the RISE process. So, if it

Chapter 6

is okay with you, let's just take a deep breath before we go on and check in on your progress and mindset.

- How do you feel about what you have learned so far?
- What are the biggest aha moments you have had so far?
- What are you most excited about now that you have learned more about visibility?

Capture your thoughts here in the book or in your notebook. You have spent time to reflect, created answers for yourself about what you want to do, and reviewed a large list of potential ideas. That is big! Cue the confetti, please! Let's do a little celebration dance here!

Notes

Chapter 7:
THE ULTIMATE BATTLE: IMPOSTOR SYNDROME

THE LATE MAYA ANGELOU, POET, singer, and civil rights activist, once said, "I have written eleven books, but each time I think, uh oh, they're going to find out now. I've run a game on everybody, and they're going to find me out."[25] Even though she won three Grammys, was nominated for a Pulitzer Prize and a Tony Award, and read a poem at the inauguration of President Clinton, she still questioned her success. Who knew that Maya Angelou—as accomplished as she was—and I both suffered from impostor syndrome?

I remember having similar thoughts when I took on my first systems project leadership role. I spent every day with these thoughts in my head: *When will they figure out that I am not ready for this role yet?* and *I don't know as much as they think I do.*

I was not an IT person by education, so I felt a bit unprepared to lead teams in this technical space. My director gave me approval to attend an IT program for businesspeople. I could

The Ultimate Battle: Impostor Syndrome

learn what was needed to lead IT projects and be ready when there was a new opportunity for a leadership role. No one at my company had ever been in a program like this, so it was great to be the first one. I was very grateful that my director believed in me and gave me the opportunity.

Fast-forward to eight months after I completed the program. I had just come back from eight weeks' maternity leave and was asked to lead a team that would build a new system using technology that we had never used before.

While I was on leave, my manager had hired consultants to work on my project and help the team learn this new technology. I had been given one consultant to mentor the team, but he only criticized them. I gave him feedback multiple times that he was there to mentor the team, not make it difficult for them to learn, but he would pull the same crap the next day. He was full of attitude and acted like a jerk to everyone.

I walked down to my director's office after another bad meeting with the consultant and shut the door. I turned around and said, "I have to give you some news." It was not normal for me to shut the door, so my director sat back in his chair and said, "Okay, let's hear it."

I told him that the consultant that was hired to mentor the team needed to go… today. I didn't ask for permission, but explained: "He isn't a mentor to anyone, and that is what he was hired to do. He is a cancer that has metastasized across the team and I need to stop it now."

My director asked, "What will that mean for the go-live date of the project?" I said, "We will miss the go-live date, but if I don't do something now, the team won't make it." (This was

Chapter 7

maybe a little overdramatic, but it felt true.) He said, "Okay, let's figure out what we need to do to get him out of here." My director didn't debate me or try to change my mind. He trusted that I knew this was the right decision. We called our HR person who helped with external consultants, and the consultant was gone in an hour. It was as if the sun had come out and all the gray clouds had disappeared. Soon, we hired a new consultant who was kind and taught everyone what they needed to know.

This was a big leadership moment for me that could have backfired. I pulled the one person who knew the most out of the project. It was a big risk. It is hard to make these tough decisions, but your team needs you to take a stand for them. Don't be afraid to do what is hard. That is what a leader needs to do in these situations. I knew this decision was the best for my team, but we would have to delay the project and I had doubts about whether that would put my team and me in jeopardy with our management.

That is the paradox when it comes to impostor syndrome. You get the work done and advocate for everyone else but doubt yourself. No one else sees that you have this challenge. On days of doubt, I remembered a quote (attributed to Eleanor Roosevelt, but not actually said or written by her—still a great quote) that one of my friends had in her cube: "No one can make you feel inferior without your permission." My director agreed with my decision, yet I still questioned myself. It was time to advocate for myself, as I had for my team. I had people around me who believed in me, and I needed to trust those beliefs when I didn't feel them myself.

The Ultimate Battle: Impostor Syndrome

Resistance

RESISTANCE SHOWED UP FOR ME when I started the business, coached my first clients, and as I wrote this book. I would tell myself, *I am not ready to be a coach yet—I just need to take additional training or practice some more and then I can do it.* Or I would write some chapters for this book, think they weren't good enough, and wonder if I could be an author. I was a coach who owned her own business and aspired to become an author. These were all firsts for me, and it was uncomfortable. My impostor thoughts told me I wasn't ready. Those thoughts created the fear and resistance inside of me.

This is what resistance looks like for high achievers who want success. To keep you safe, impostor syndrome keeps you out of action. Remember what I shared in Chapter 3 about what I did to prepare for my "New Business"? I told myself the tasks of creating my business name, website, and new business cards were the safe, easy things I had to do first so clients would see that I am credible. That story wasn't true, though—that was resistance and fear. I know coaches who do nothing on social media and don't have websites. It was my fear and insecurity about this new world of coaching and business ownership that led me to focus on the busy, hide-behind-the-computer work instead of the get-out-there-and-meet-some-clients work I should have been doing.

I have learned a lot more about how resistance works since that time. In Chapter 5, I shared how new experiences make us uncomfortable because they push us to grow. Do you know what tells you that you are about to grow? The physical reaction in your stomach, chest, or head and that loudmouthed critic in your mind who says harsh words to keep you safe. Steven Pressfield, author of *The War of Art: Winning the Inner Creative Battle,* said, "The more Resistance you experience, the more important your unmanifested art/project/enterprise is to you—and the more gratification you feel when you finally do it."[26] How many people experience resistance and stop themselves from any forward progress when success is right around the corner? They hold themselves back and miss out on opportunities.

I had a choice to make as I went through those firsts: Either lean into the fear and resistance or stay stuck. Remember when I said I had been told that you should do what scares you the most? I had to trust that what I was about to do was right for me and it was okay if I made mistakes. I would learn from them, adjust, and try again the next day. When I saw starting my own coaching business as an experiment instead of an all-or-nothing decision, it became easier for me to move forward. I look back now and see that I could have fallen into the trap of resistance. I would have missed out on so many great experiences. Trust that you already have what you need to do what you want, and you will build upon that foundation as you go or ask for help from others if you need it.

I'm Not Good Enough

As the company went through multiple layoff cycles after I left, I noticed smart and capable leaders who suddenly seemed a bit lost. They had been with the company for a long time and weren't sure how to navigate this new career transition experience. They tended to apply for jobs at levels that were at or below their previous position. They thought that they weren't good enough to apply for higher-level roles and still believed the story their former leaders had told them, that to move to the next level meant they had to do more. They didn't know that, in many cases, those managers had no place for them to progress to and needed to keep them motivated. That is why they were told to do more, not because they weren't good enough.

When I talked to these recently laid-off leaders, I could hear the doubt and fear in their voices. I redirected our conversations to focus on the great results they had achieved, and encouraged them to apply for roles that were at least one level higher than their last jobs. This was their opportunity to go to the next level and leverage what they could do at other companies. They could let go of the old stories that previous managers had told them and create new stories that they could use in interviews. As they found new roles, they shared updates with me. I heard comments like, "I haven't done that much yet, and they think I am a rock star! Imagine when I show them all that I can do, they will be blown away!" They had always been rock stars, but they hadn't believed it or had the opportunity to show it before. This transition was a chance for them to see that they were more than good enough.

How Does Impostor Syndrome Start?

I WAS THE FIRSTBORN AND I wanted my parents to be proud of me. The truth is, I wanted to please my family and have their approval. I continued to strive for perfection with my teachers and then, as an adult, with my managers. Does this sound familiar for you, too? I grew accustomed to external validation, and without it I felt as if I had failed in some way. Without the pat on the back, I had no barometer to tell me how I was performing. I hadn't learned how to trust myself and find the validation inside.

People with impostor syndrome are overachievers who have strong values, and they want to master things. Impostor syndrome rises to the surface when they want to be good at something and avoid failure. If they can't do it well, then maybe they shouldn't even try. If they don't write that article or make that speech, no one can see them; therefore, they won't fail.

Such self-critical thoughts, and comparing yourself to others, can make you feel as if you don't belong and aren't good enough. And if you judge and criticize yourself, you prevent anyone else from doing it to you first. You remain perfect in their eyes. (Win-win, right? Sure, if you want to stay right where you are.)

"No matter how successful someone is on the outside, or how much external evidence there is of their skills or competence, people with impostor syndrome are convinced that they don't deserve the success they have achieved, and it impacts over 70 percent of people in the US at some point in their career," Vanessa Van Edwards wrote in a recent blog post for *Science of People*.[27]

Impostor syndrome was first identified back in 1978 in an article titled "The Impostor Phenomenon in High Achieving Women: Dynamics and Therapeutic Intervention"[28] by Dr. Pauline R. Clance and Dr. Suzanne A. Imes. The article highlighted how this challenge impacts overachieving women who try to fit in and be perfect, and mentions multiple examples of intelligent women who diminished their high-level roles as mistakes, luck, or due to the fact that someone hadn't yet figured out that they didn't belong where they were.

A New Role Can Create Impostor Syndrome

LET ME SHARE THIS STORY with you of one of my peers, Rachel, as she walked into her office recently after receiving a promotion. Her eyes lit up with excitement as she relayed to me how she stopped to stare at her name on the wall outside of her new office. "Rachel Harris," she read, but it still didn't seem real that it was there. As she turned the corner, she knew what she would see: a cherrywood desk and credenza, two chairs, and a whiteboard hidden behind cherrywood doors. She looked down at the bookcase and ran her hand over its smooth surface. She had thought about every detail of the office ever since she got the job—how she would decorate it, where she would put her stuff and display the pictures of her family. All of this was now hers! This office was a symbol of so much work and time devoted to the company over the years. She had worked so hard, and it had paid off with the promotion she'd just received. So why did she close the door to her new office and feel as if there must be some mistake?

What Rachel experienced is very common. New experiences tend to stir excitement, but also self-doubt. You don't want to fail or let anyone down. You don't want to disappoint them. Though you have had success in the past, you discount those situations as flukes or don't see them as similar to the present situation. Fear can overtake you and keep you from achieving your true potential.

Chapter 7

Rachel felt pretty much the same as she did before the promotion, but people treated her differently now. Somehow the title and an office made everyone assume that she had joined some secret management club and had all the answers. She felt so much pressure, she couldn't enjoy the moment. All the messages in her head were full of self-doubt: *I can't believe they gave me this job. What happens when they find out I don't know what to do? I will fail, and everyone will know I am just an impostor.*

Overachievers tend to focus on negative thoughts amidst all the positive ones. What happened the last time you started something new? Were your thoughts positive and full of confidence, or were they negative and filled with self-doubt? For some people, it is a mixture of both.

Impostor syndrome can manifest in different ways for each person. How do you know if you have impostor syndrome? Listen to your thoughts and pay attention to how you answer these questions: Do you compare yourself to others and feel as if you aren't good enough? Do you procrastinate, or self-sabotage to avoid criticism? Are you a people-pleaser? Do you breach your own boundaries to make others happy at the cost of *your* happiness? Do you fail to respond when people diminish you or your work? Do you put on a "mask" and become what everyone else wants you to be?

If you answered yes to these questions, then welcome to the impostor syndrome club! Believe me, I know this may be tough to digest. This next section will help you realize that you aren't alone, and offer insight into how I coach people who have impostor syndrome. Sometimes it helps to see others' experiences in order to recognize your own.

The Ultimate Battle: Impostor Syndrome

Is Everyone Impacted by Impostor Syndrome?

MOST PEOPLE ASSUME THAT IMPOSTOR syndrome only impacts women. This isn't true at all. An Oscar-winning actor who has made seventy films and TV shows has impostor syndrome. "No matter what we've done, there comes a point where you think, 'How did I get here? When are they going to discover that I am, in fact, a fraud and take everything away from me?'" Tom Hanks, a highly awarded actor, said that on NPR's *Fresh Air* podcast in 2016.[29]

In an interview with the *Baltimore Business Journal*, Dr. Pauline Rose Clance, who first began the study of the impostor phenomenon, said that she had expected to find that it affected more women than men. "But feeling like an impostor seems to happen with both men and women," Clance said. "Decades ago, men were less open to talking about it, but their experience of the phenomenon has come out through anonymous surveys."[30]

"There isn't much research out there on the causes of the impostor phenomenon, but it can be attributed to a mix of nature and nurture. Children who have been told to not bring attention to themselves or to not feel that they are better than others are predisposed to impostor syndrome, as are firstborn children, due to the expectations of success placed on them as youngsters," Vanessa Van Edwards writes.[31]

I had all three of these experiences—the trifecta of impostor syndrome—and didn't win a prize, although I guess I am in the club with Oscar-winning actors and millions of others. That is something, right?

Chapter 7

The Traits of Impostor Syndrome

THERE ARE MULTIPLE PERSONALITY TRAITS associated with impostor syndrome. Since the syndrome was first identified, there have been various names for each of these traits. I chose to create some alternate names which I think describe them more realistically than the psychological terms can.

Each trait description below includes a client situation, so you can see how it impacts them; gives you a peek inside a coaching session; and shares the suggestions that I offered the client, which could be useful to you if you are impacted by it. You will see how there can be an overlap between the different traits and behaviors. Keep an open mind as you read each scenario and ask yourself which ones you identify with and how they impact you the most. At the end of each section, I will provide some suggestions for shifting your behaviors.

Agreeable Accommodator (a.k.a. People-Pleaser)

JULIE'S FRIEND MICHAEL ASKED HER to go to dinner with him. As he said the words, she thought to herself: *I have a million things to do, so I should say no—but then he will be upset with me.* She said yes, though she didn't want to go. Julie is a people-pleaser and, in her view, it is more important to make her friend happy and say yes than it is to put herself first and say no. She is always agreeable and accommodates other people's needs before her own. She volunteers to take on more work, though she has limited bandwidth. Her justification is that it will get her some bonus points come performance review time.

The Ultimate Battle: Impostor Syndrome

Her energy is focused in so many directions, and her stress level is high. She doesn't prioritize herself at work or at home. Her heart is in the right place—she makes sure everyone else is happy and taken care of—but she needs to prioritize herself more than anyone else.

Julie had a goal to be more visible, but when I talked to her about what she wanted for herself, she said, "I do want that, but I can't think about *how* to be visible. I'm a manager who has too much to juggle with such a massive workload right now."

I asked her, "Could you delegate your work to anyone else, or talk to your boss about how to reprioritize?"

She began to speak faster as she said, "My boss depends on me and I like that he does. He relies on me to take on extra work so he can work on strategy for our department. I can take on a large workload, and although I have to put in a lot of hours, my team and I find a way to get it done."

Her answers are classic for someone who accommodates everyone else. Being needed fulfills something inside Julie. She has a strong work ethic, wants to be relied on by others and will do whatever it takes to put others first, though it is to her and her team's detriment.

"Why it is more important for your boss to have time for strategy than you, when you also have a team?" I asked. Her face was full of admiration as she replied, "He leads this whole organization, and it is more important for him to focus on his work and communication. My team and I are here to support him so that he can do what he needs to do."

I said, "Your self-sacrifice is noble, but do you think that helps your leadership team see you as a leader or a doer?" She crossed her arms when she answered, "When you put it like

Chapter 7

that, I am a doer." I asked her if I could share an observation with her. She nodded her head in agreement. I continued, "You put your boss on a pedestal, and that means that you defer to him to take on more. Is that how you want to show up as a leader for yourself and your team? How would it look if you delegated more to your team to help them develop their skills and don't take on everything so you have the time to create visibility for yourself?" She said, "I didn't believe I had the option to say no. I am intrigued to try these shifts and make my life less crazy."

As we continued to coach together, Julie gained more awareness of her agreeable behaviors and where she accommodated too much. She could see that these habits didn't serve her or her team.

Paulo Coelho, author of *The Alchemist* and many other books, said, "When you say yes to others, make sure you are not saying no to yourself."[32] It was a big step for Julie to reflect before she said yes to someone. It will take her time to learn how to put herself first. Saying no is a challenge for people who put others first, so I gave her three suggestions for how to do it:

1. "Thank you for the invitation, but I'm not available to attend the movie tonight." You don't have to explain anything, only that you aren't available.

2. If you are asked to help on another project when your plate is already full, try: "I would love to help on that project, but I have a full workload right now. If I complete something soon, I will let you know."

3. Identify three activities that you would like to do for yourself. Create a self-care routine that you can stick with every week to ensure that you fill your cup before you offer to help someone else.

Notice that in these examples, no apologies are used. You don't have to apologize when you say no to someone else. You have the choice to do what is right for you in your personal and professional life. Use your voice to ask for what you want and set boundaries so you can have time to accomplish your goals. If Julie puts herself first when something doesn't work for her, it will help her to focus on herself and not on the accommodations for others.

Just Can't Say No (a.k.a. No Boundaries)

NANCY FELT AS IF SHE had to be the superwoman in all areas of her life. She was married with two kids and had major work responsibilities that seemed to grow each month. She felt that she needed to be available for work all the time and would not ask for help—she didn't want to tell people that she couldn't do something or let anyone down. She blocked out space in her calendar at work, but if someone asked for a meeting with her, she would give them her time. She wanted to be liked, but knew in her heart that people took advantage of her. Although it took a toll on her, she thought she could do it all.

The ability to say no and create limits can reduce the overwhelm and allow you to make decisions about where and how you spend your time. It is good to spend time doing what you want for yourself, but it made Nancy feel guilty.

Chapter 7

Nancy had started to work on a plan to gain more visibility and then stopped. "What caused you to stop the progress on your plan?" I asked. She said, "I have too many meetings on my calendar. I get new projects thrown at me and I am overwhelmed."

"What have you done to maintain the limits on your time?" Nancy said, "I haven't been strong enough to say no. When people want to meet with me, I feel as if I let them down if I say I can't meet with them at that time. I don't want them to say I am not helpful."

"Has anyone ever told you that you aren't helpful?" I replied. She smiled at me. "No, they haven't," she said. "Would it be helpful for you to offer some alternative times to meet instead of accepting a meeting that doesn't work for you?" She nodded her head yes. I then asked, "What are the most important meetings that you have, and who are they with?" Nancy said, "My clients and my managers. I prioritize those first."

I nodded in agreement. "Those are important meetings for you to attend. Do you think that your time is less valuable than that of anyone else who wants to meet with you?" She had been focused on the floor as I asked her the question. She looked up at me with tears in her eyes and responded, "I have put myself at the back of the line in all areas of my life and my career. I don't want that to be true for me anymore." She sat up straighter in her chair with this moment of clarity. I asked her what she was thinking. She said, "I created that story in my head that I couldn't say no. I get to make the decisions about how to spend my time, and it is as valuable as other people's time." It was almost as if she had written a new permission slip for herself to say no and maintain her boundaries.

The Ultimate Battle: Impostor Syndrome

Brené Brown says, "Daring to set boundaries is about having the courage to love ourselves even when we risk disappointing others."[33] Nancy allowed others into her space so she wouldn't be judged and excluded. She was overwhelmed and had no time left for herself, her goals, or anything else. We identified some ways that she could preserve and allocate her time:

1. Be ruthless with your calendar and the time that you have blocked off to work on your goals. Your time is just as valuable and important as any meeting with your boss or clients.

2. Say no to whatever is not in line with your goals and values. You get to come first, always. You can't help others until you help yourself. (Use the suggestions in the agreeable accommodators section if you need ideas for how to say no.)

3. Make yourself a priority:
   a. Stay out of other people's issues and plans. Focus on your own plan.
   b. Focus on your needs versus what everyone else wants from you (be aware that you will be tempted to focus on others, because that is still a habit).
   c. Choose to do what brings you joy each day.

4. Focus on two to three things you can do toward your goals each day, not your entire list.
   a. Don't try to take on too much each day (and then accomplish nothing).

Chapter 7

    b. Complete two to three things each day to give yourself a sense of satisfaction and accomplishment.

The inability to say no and the willingness to accommodate others are tightly intertwined. When you are challenged with both traits, it is good to work on them together so you have more awareness and can limit how they will impact you. You are not selfish. Prioritizing yourself gives you what you need so that you can help whomever you choose.

I didn't know what the word "self-care" meant before someone coached me on it about eleven years ago. I had no idea that I was always in survival mode or that there were other options that would be better for me and therefore better for my family. I thought that I was being a good wife and mother by putting them first, but that caused me to abandon myself—which wasn't good for me or for them. I had to learn how to put myself first and figure out what self-care meant for me. A focus on my own self-care has made such a difference for my mindset and mental health. If you are similar to me and have no idea what to do in the self-care space, then google "ideas for self-care." Choose a few ideas to try out and see if they are helpful for you!

One last thought on this from your virtual coach. How many times have you made promises to someone else and kept them? I bet you do that all the time. What if you make promises to yourself and keep those instead? You are worth it!

Image Judger (a.k.a. Comparer)

TOM WAS SOMEONE WHO APPEARED to have it all together. He dressed well, worked out, and had a great job and family.

Inside, however, he compared himself to his friends and looked over his shoulder at the competition. It was necessary for him to create visibility for the organization as part of his role, but he wasn't sure if he was ready for that. He preferred to stay in the office and be with his team instead. He was challenged to set an example as a senior leader in a situation that entailed a lot of responsibility. He was insecure and held himself back from other opportunities because he wasn't sure he was ready. He didn't feel as if he was as good as the competitors that he admired.

How does this self-judgment begin? Remember, it started when we were young. We were rated in school, in sports, and at home. Statistics tracked our grades and sports achievements, and our parents judged our accomplishments against those of our siblings and friends.

Within companies, we are rated on our performance and potential. Companies are judged in comparison to their competition. Neighbors compete with status symbols. It is time to stop the merry-go-round of judgment and comparison. It is a drain on our energy and makes us unhappy.

Tom and I met for an online coaching call. I asked him, "What progress have you made on your external and internal visibility goals?"

He looked down at the floor and said, "I can see all these other people who I know are visible and I don't know why I can't do it. I feel like a fraud and that I will be judged."

I asked, "Who would judge you?"

He threw his hands up in the air as he said, "I don't know, my team or clients maybe. I guess I worry about other people's approval too much."

Chapter 7

I asked if I could share a quote with him. He nodded for me to continue. I quoted Lao Tzu: "Care about people's approval and you will be their prisoner."[34] I asked him to think about that and then said, "Do you want to give all the power you have to someone else? You can't control what they think or what they do. All you can do is control your own thoughts and behaviors."

Then I asked, "If you weren't worried about what anyone else thought of you, what could you accomplish toward your visibility goals?"

He pondered for a minute and then his face lit up. It was as if the ideas that had been locked up inside of him were suddenly released. He responded, "I would find some new ways to connect more with my team, do more networking with some of the local businesspeople, attend more conferences, and make more speeches."

"Those are great ways for you to get visibility. Is there any obstacle that could prevent you from completing these ideas?"

Tom said, "Nothing. I can see that I was more concerned about what other people thought than with what I want to do. I wasn't trusting myself. I was the only one holding me back. That doesn't help my company or me at all."

He was more focused on external validation than self-trust. His preoccupation with what other people thought of him wasted his time and took energy from where he wanted to spend it—with the team and the business. And it made him feel as if he wasn't good enough. He was successful, but it never felt like enough.

This is a journey and there is no scorecard. Don't compare yourself to others and put them on a pedestal. Stay on your own path and don't worry about the competition.

The Ultimate Battle: Impostor Syndrome

We talked about some ways Tom could stop the comparison and self-judgment:

1. Author Olin Miller said, "You probably wouldn't worry about what people think of you if you could know how seldom they do."[35] Would it change your conversations and actions if you remembered that the people you interact with don't think about you?

2. Take small steps. Trust your gut, take risks, make decisions, and realize that you know what to do. As your confidence grows, you will make bigger decisions and what other people do won't be a concern for you anymore.

3. Do you compare your inside with others' outsides? Look at social media and you will see that everyone appears to have it all together. Is the life they show on social media real or a fictional portrayal? Everyone has both bad and good stuff in their life, and no one is perfect. Let me say that again: No one is perfect! Focus on your own unique value and strengths that you bring to the world. You have a responsibility to do that for yourself. How can you continue to share those gifts and make them visible, both to help yourself and support anyone who needs them?

Everyone wants to be seen in a positive way and recognized for doing well in their jobs, but how much of your time is spent focused on what your management or others think of you?

Chapter 7

When the day goes well, you may not think about it too much at all. It becomes a challenge when you get feedback on an issue or are criticized for how you handled a situation. You start to watch what you do and say all the time. This can cause you to hide and it may limit your productivity and blur your focus.

You can only control what you do every day. If you want to make a change, then do it. Don't do it for someone else, do it for yourself. Focus on yourself and the great gifts that are unique to you. Do the best you can and believe in yourself. It has been said that "comparison is the thief of joy." Time is too short to spend focused on everyone else.

Diminished and Devalued (a.k.a. Plays Small)

CAROL RECEIVED FEEDBACK FROM HER manager that she and her team had done a great job on the new project Carol had led. She didn't want to make too much of it and said, "Thanks, it was not a big deal, we were just doing our job." This project took two years to implement, and her team had done it with minimal issues. That is a big deal, but when Carol said it wasn't, she devalued what she and her team had just accomplished. All that hard work they did deserved recognition.

Carol was great at execution, but she stayed in the background. When people made comments that she disagreed with, she wouldn't confront them. She struggled to push back with people who had stronger personalities when they called her out in disagreement. She second-guessed herself and assumed they were right; she buried her responses and didn't say a word.

Carol knew she could do more but wasn't sure how to get past this challenge. We talked about ways that she could create more opportunities for herself, but she struggled to implement any of the ideas.

I asked her, "You put together a list of goals for yourself that require you to be out in front. Do you want to do this?"

She responded, "I hate to be the center of attention. I prefer to stay in the background, so I don't get judged."

I let that comment sit in silence for a few moments before I replied in a quiet tone, "Who would judge you, and why?"

As she recalled previous traumatic experiences, her eyes became sad. "I have seen others ridiculed when they have an opinion that conflicts with my management," Carol said. "On the other hand, if I do well, then I get teased by my peers. I can't win no matter what I do. I don't want to risk the embarrassment, so I avoid it."

I could see that it was hard for her to stand out, and that explained why she preferred to blend in with the group and belong. I decided to go in a different direction when I asked her, "Who do you work with whom you admire, and what do they do well?"

She smiled as she thought about her answer. "My friend Debbie is great at this stuff. She sells her ideas, gets results, and builds relationships. I have learned a lot from her."

I said, "I can see that you admire her. What would she say that you do well?"

She said, "Debbie would say that I get results and build relationships, too."

"So it isn't just Debbie who does things well—you do, too. What actions could you take to be just ten percent more visible when you do those things? A small number of steps still move you in the right direction." We talked about the small steps she could take for visibility and how she could prepare herself to respond when there were disagreements or if she was teased by some of her peers.

Carol justified why she should be in the background and let others stand out instead. I wanted her to see that others stand out with the same skills that she has, and hoped that realization would give her an opportunity to increase what she does out front. She put herself down before others could do it. She chose invisibility for herself and for her team. She wanted to be recognized, but she was fearful of standing out and wouldn't accept recognition.

Once we talked about the ways that Carol hid, she could see that it also happened in her personal life. Tanya Geisler, speaker, coach, and host of the podcast *Ready Enough*, is an impostor syndrome expert. She says, "The thing you are afraid of being criticized for is most likely the thing you have not yet accepted about yourself. The thing you are most wanting praise for is the thing you don't feel like you CAN accept yet."[36] It was going to take time to help Carol shift her mindset, but we started with some suggestions to help her value herself and build her confidence.

1. Being part of a supportive group is important in helping you to eliminate your fears of judgment. Find the people who can be a part of your group and help lift you up with no strings attached.

The Ultimate Battle: Impostor Syndrome

2. When someone says you have done something great, believe them. Accept the compliment with, at minimum, a simple thank you. Allow yourself to enjoy the accomplishment and be proud of yourself.

3. When someone puts you down or criticizes what you have done, understand that those comments are about them, not you. They may be jealous, or afraid to take the same risks. It is easier for them to project their fears than face them. You don't need to hide because of what someone else says to you. You get to choose what to believe. Don't allow yourself to be devalued. Remember, those thoughts become true if you let them. Shine bright regardless of what anyone says—you deserve this!

Judgment and devaluation work together to stop you from doing what you want to do. That only happens if you let it, though. You get to make another choice and remember what you have already accomplished. It is great to let others see the value you bring, but at this point, it is more important that you see this for yourself. This is your chance to acknowledge your own value and let go of the clutter in your head.

This one has been a challenge for me, too. Each of these traits have impacted me at one point or another, but this one was a personal blind spot. I shared a related experience with my coach, and through that conversation, I could see that I had let the other person devalue me and it had decreased my confidence. Now that I saw how that could happen, I remained aware of it.

If this trait impacts you, be brave and bold. Identify someone you admire and act as they would until you get more comfortable. We all have a responsibility to share our value with others, every single day.

Delayer and Avoider (a.k.a. Procrastinator)

AARON ALWAYS FOUND A WAY to delay the work he didn't want to do, although, for as long as he could remember, he still managed to get things done at the last minute. He would tell people that he worked well under pressure as if it was a badge of accomplishment. Though he always finished his work by the deadline, he often wondered what he could create if he took the time to spread the work over a longer timeframe instead. Was this a habit, or something else? As Aaron started to look at his tendency to avoid and delay, he realized that it happened in more places in his life than he'd thought. He put off decisions, delayed making connections with people, and avoided focusing on his goals. He was busy, but was he busy in the right areas?

The most common impostor trait of overachievers is avoidance. Elizabeth Gilbert says, "Perfectionism stops people from completing their work, yes—but it often stops people from beginning their work which is worse. Perfectionists often decide in advance that the end-product is never going to be satisfactory, so they don't bother trying to be creative in the first place."[37] Delay and avoidance will (temporarily) help you avoid judgment, criticism, or failure. They keep you safe, but may not help you do what you want, or at the highest quality due to lack of time.

Aaron struggled with stopping this pattern so he could be visible as a leader in the ways he wanted to be.

The Ultimate Battle: Impostor Syndrome

He ran his hands through his hair nervously and said, "I am not sure what stops me from the work I need to do." For example, I want to connect with more people, but I am afraid that I will say the wrong thing, so I never meet with them." I replied, "Have you had conversations where you have said the wrong thing?" He laughed and said, "No, I guess I haven't." I wondered if he was feeling insecure. "Are these people intimidating to you in some way?" He got up and began to pace the room as he said, "They do have a lot of influence and their opinion about me is important to my career."

"Do you feel as if you need to have the perfect conversation?" I asked.

He looked away when he responded. "That may be true. I worry that I will ruin my credibility with these connections if I don't do well, and then I won't have another chance."

I asked, "Do you think that they expect you to have a perfect conversation with them?"

"No, they don't," he replied. I continued, "Is it true that you wouldn't have another chance if you did happen to say something that wasn't perfect?" He stopped pacing and stood behind his chair. "No. I would clarify the mistake with them if I made one."

I asked the next question: "What do you think they do expect?"

Aaron responded, "They want to meet with me and have a good conversation."

"Would you be able to do that without feeling the pressure you felt earlier?" I asked.

Aaron sat back down and looked visibly relieved as he thought about it for a minute and said, "Yes. I was more worried about the outcome and what they would think of me than how enjoyable a conversation with them could be. If I never meet with them, then they won't know who I am. We are human beings having a conversation and no one is better than the other person. If I focus on that, there is no pressure anymore—I can be myself and focus on the conversation. I am excited to meet with them."

Brené Brown said, "You can't do anything brave if you are wearing the straightjacket of what will people think."[38] The fear of failure or judgment can overpower you, and it held Aaron back from connecting with other people. With this type of impostor syndrome more than any other, people will use any means possible to stop themselves from doing something that makes them feel vulnerable to judgment or criticism.

Something I have caught myself doing when I want to avoid something hard or that I don't want to do is sit down to watch a show on Netflix—with the best intentions to only watch one episode. Hours later, I am into the second season of the show and I can't seem to stop! When this happens, it is called "putting oneself to sleep" or "numbing" so that you avoid whatever you need to do. It can happen at work, also. You sit down to talk to someone about one situation and then, before you realize it, an hour or two are gone. Social media is another culprit that steals your time and sucks you in so you don't accomplish what is necessary.

Avoidance is a pattern of behavior that is used to delay action, but now that you know that, it is important to look below the surface so you can address its root cause.

Aaron and I talked about the types of situations where he might avoid his action plan or other deliverables. I asked him

The Ultimate Battle: Impostor Syndrome

if I could share an observation with him. He nodded and I continued, "If you want to change how you are perceived, the only way to do that is to be out in front. Create a system that will help you break through your avoidance behaviors. It will be the most important thing you do."

Here are some of the ways that we discussed he might do that:

1. You have your plan, and you know what to do. Take the first step to accomplish at least one action in your plan. That first step will spur you into further action, and you will want to keep up the momentum. Identify a deadline and have someone hold you accountable.

2. Think about what you avoid. What does the avoidance cost you? Will you miss out on a promotion, an opportunity to lead a team, or a chance to learn a new skill? For example, if you have already been given feedback to shift your behavior, then what could happen if you don't address it?

3. People who use distractions as avoidance do it for a reason. Taking action helps you move forward. Set a timer to work on an activity for thirty minutes. Shut everything else off and focus for that half hour. Doing this regularly will allow you to make headway on your actions in short sprints; there is no need to feel overwhelmed. You can also create a rewards-based system for yourself. Rewards don't have to come from other

people. When you accomplish work on your goal, give yourself a reward.

Avoidance may be a habit that you learned in high school or college, and back then, it worked for you. You put off an assignment until the last minute, but you made your deadline. Aaron struggled because he had no deadlines; he could self-sabotage and avoid what he said he wanted to do forever. He faced resistance and fear that caused him to move into a mode of inaction.

However, inaction has consequences that must be faced sooner or later. If Aaron wanted to achieve his goals, he had to start with some form of action. It sounds so simple, but as someone who has lived through it, I know that the challenge is real. Aaron began to implement the suggestions above, and that gave him the motivation to make great progress on his goals.

Criticism Avoider (a.k.a. Perfectionist)

ASHLEY WAS A DIRECTOR IN a company and wanted to move into a VP role. She worked a lot of hours at the office, then went home and did what needed to be done there, too. She was proud to do it all and didn't ask for help. She set high standards for herself, and she had also set them for her team. It was important to her that things were done right. However, the more she tried to control what happened, the more she struggled to manage it all. She was stressed out and slept very little. She knew this wasn't sustainable, but she was the breadwinner of the family and felt so much pressure to keep it all together. In her mind, there was no choice but to play the game at work and be what they wanted her to be in order to be successful. Inside, though, she felt like a failure. This wasn't the example she wanted to set for her team at work or for her kids. Her current approach would have to change if she wanted to achieve a promotion that would bring more responsibilities.

Brené Brown breaks down perfectionism in this way: "We struggle with perfectionism in areas where we feel most vulnerable to shame. Perfectionism is a 20-ton shield that we carry around hoping it will keep us from being hurt, when in truth what it does is it keeps us from being seen. It is a way of thinking that says that if I look perfect, live perfect, work perfect, I can avoid or minimize criticism, blame and ridicule."[39] Perfection is an illusion and a slippery slope. Whatever you do, it never seems to be quite good enough. The focus is always on other people and what they think. You wear a mask that shows them what they want to see, not you, the person who exists away from the office.

Ashley worked with me on ways to position herself for the VP role that she wanted. When we met, I could see the stress all over her face. She couldn't sit still. She looked at her watch multiple times and played with her bracelets. I could see the toll that perfectionism had taken on her.

"How is your work and home life?" I asked.

She answered, "I try my best, but I feel like a failure all the way around. I can't seem to do anything right and there isn't enough of me to go around."

I asked, "Did someone tell you that you are a failure?"

"No," she said. "Not at all. My work thinks I am great, but I have to juggle so much right now. I'm stressed out and I know I will fail soon."

Chapter 7

"What would help you have more time?" I asked.

She brainstormed some ideas. "I could delegate more to my team, ask for help at home from my husband and kids, and look at what I have to do at work and prioritize two or three items each day instead of my whole to-do list."

"Those are all good ideas," I said. "If you implemented them, would it be enough to help you?"

Ashley began to cry. She sat there with tears streaming down her face. She said, "No, those would help, but they wouldn't be enough. To be honest, I am worried about what everyone else thinks of me. I want them to think that I do a good job. I want to be perfect and control what happens at work and at home."

I waited for a minute before I asked her, "How would it be for you if you didn't worry about what everyone else thought of you?"

Although there were still tears in her eyes, she thought about it for a minute and then her face brightened as she smiled. "It would be a huge relief! I have knots in my stomach all the time at work and then I bring all that home. I could let all that go and just be me."

"You have carried around this story that you have to be perfect for a long time now. What if that story didn't exist anymore? What could the new story be instead?"

Ashley sat up tall and straightened her jacket. She spoke with confidence when she said, "I am great just as I am right now. I don't have to be perfect. It is good to ask for help from others, and though they do things differently than I do, it is all right."

I replied to her, "How would it be to let them see the imperfect you right now?"

The Ultimate Battle: Impostor Syndrome

She relaxed her shoulders, and I could see the invisible weight she carried start to lift a little bit as she said, "It would be an adjustment for me, but I want to set an example for my kids and my team. They need to know that it is okay to be 'perfectly imperfect'"—here she made air quotes—"and accept yourself."

It is one thing to strive for perfection, but it is unrealistic to demand it of yourself and others. About this, Brené Brown says, "Many people think of perfectionism as striving to be your best, but it is not about self-improvement; it's about earning approval and acceptance."[40] Ashley had focused on everyone else and lost sight of what she wanted for herself. The belief that she needed more external validation had consumed her thoughts and impacted how she behaved. Now she felt empowered to focus on what she wanted and no longer needed everyone else's approval and acceptance.

When you decide not to care what other people think, the desire to be perfect also falls away. Focus on yourself, trust that you have the answers to know what to do, and if you need help, ask for it. Ashley and I discussed some strategies that she could focus on:

1. Listen to the words that you use with others or the self-talk that goes on in your own head. Do you expect that you will do everything right every time? Do you expect everyone else to do this as well?

2. Do your best and seek out excellence, but not perfection. Do you spend too much time on details that aren't that important? How much is your time worth? Does it make sense to spend more time on this one action or move on

to the next one? Leverage the 80/20 rule. Is 80 percent good enough for people to get what they need, or is it truly worth the time spent to gain another 20 percent? Have you done your best? Give yourself permission to say that you have done this with excellence and your time is better spent on something else now.

3. Imagine how different your life would be if you didn't try to be perfect. What if you accepted yourself, wherever you are at this moment? What if you did what you loved and it gave you a sense of purpose? You would get out of bed every day excited to go to work and do what you love! You wouldn't care what others thought, because you'd know deep inside that this is what you are supposed to do.

4. Brené Brown says that "Perfectionism is not the same thing as striving to be our best. Perfectionism is not about healthy achievement and growth; it's a shield."[41] Have you ever thought that you might have a shield you use to avoid criticism? Your shield may be procrastination, self-sabotage, or criticism of others. Watch to see when and where you use your shield. Imagine how your life would be without that heavy burden of armor to carry around all the time.

In her article "Retiring Perfectionism," Jess Winans, writer, speaker, and coach, said, "Shaming yourself into believing that you are inadequate and unworthy of love, success, or happiness because you do not fit into the mold that you have developed in your mind. When you are a perfectionist, your own vision of yourself becomes so distorted that every compliment dealt to you is turned into a new standard that you must overcome or a new goal you must achieve."[42]

It may seem as if the best approach is never to do anything wrong, but this is an illusion, not to mention impossible. It is a burden, and it makes you miserable. Imagine someone arising from bed one day and realizing how much time they have wasted trying to be perfect. What if they had accepted themselves as they were, let go of what others thought, and lived a happy life?

Do you remember when you were a child and saw something new to try? You did it without questioning yourself. Did you care if others thought it was a good idea? Did you ask someone if it was okay to do it? No, you just did it! When did it become more important to believe what others thought of us than it was to be ourselves? Why do we feel that we aren't already great right now? Why do we think that the actions we take have to be done in a certain way?

Society has painted this version of how people should be and what we should do. It is an impossible ideal, and social media just magnifies it and makes it worse. Perfectionism causes people to hide, avoid criticism, and view mistakes in a negative way. Mistakes are what help you learn the most! In my own experience, I thought everyone else had expectations of me and that I was supposed to deliver everything on the invisible list that ran in my head. The truth is that no one else expected perfection of me. I put that on myself. The acceptance of who I am and that I am enough was a huge first step.

Chapter 7

Give yourself permission to let go of all these expectations, accept yourself for who and where you are in this moment, and know that you have all you need to be successful right now. Be happy and empowered to make your own life choices.

I hope this chapter gave you some new insights that will help prepare you for any impostor obstacles. Think about how to plan for any of these challenges should they happen when you perform your new visibility actions.

In the next chapter, we will get back to the RISE process, and in step three you will get to select the ideas that you want to include in your plan, determine how you will measure success, and decide who you will ask to give you feedback as you try out these new actions. Notice that I used the words "get to" at the beginning of the previous sentence, not "have to." That was intentional. You get to decide if you want to view this plan as a fun adventure or a difficult chore. If you see it as a difficult chore, you may want to ask yourself why you feel that way and do some reflection before you continue. It is fine to take some time to understand where the feeling comes from, so you don't quit on yourself. Once you are ready, you can join us in the next chapter.

Nicole is ready to go to step three to select her ideas. Are you ready to select your ideas, too?

Actions

1. Which of the impostor syndrome traits resonate with you the most? Did you have more than one? (It is common to have some that overlap, and different traits will tend to show up in different situations.) Write out

The Ultimate Battle: Impostor Syndrome

which of the identified strategies you will leverage to help you notice and avoid expressing these traits.

2. Write down the ways that you will ensure these impostor syndrome traits don't sabotage you as you work on the visibility actions in your plan.

Notes

RISE STEP THREE: SELECT

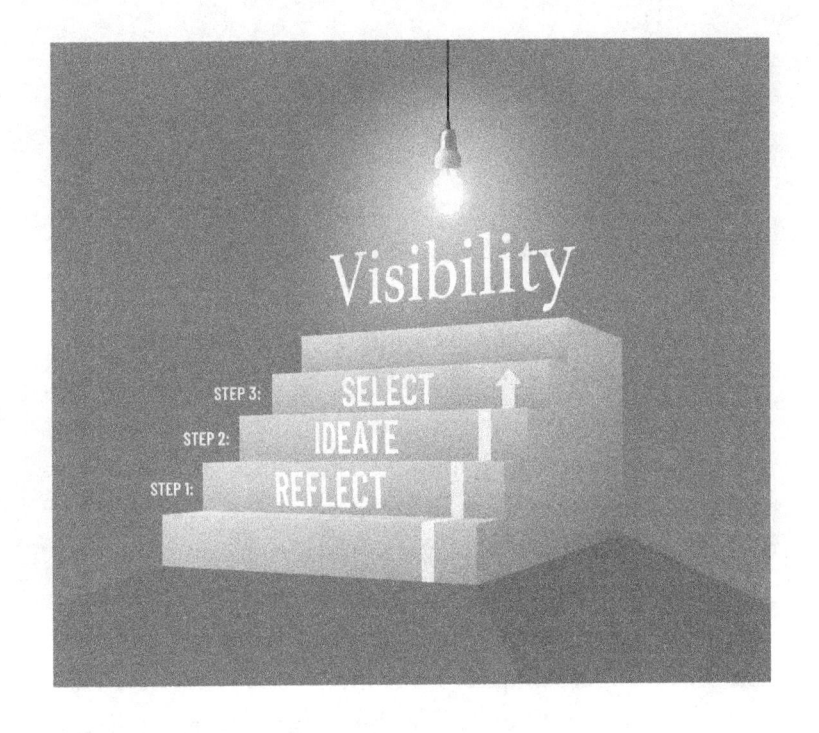

Chapter 8:
IT'S DRAFT DAY!

"WITH THE FIRST PICK OF the 2021 NFL Draft, the Chicago Bears select…" *I know they don't have the number one pick, but they are my favorite team… a girl can dream!*

If you haven't watched the National Football League (NFL) draft new players before, this is what the NFL commissioner says onstage just before he reads the name of that number one player from the card he holds. Everyone holds their breath in suspense and waits to hear him read that name. The team that selects that number one player looks at every angle of their decision when they pick the number one player to ensure that they make the best choice. The salary and bonus that a number one pick receives comprise more money than they have ever seen, and the team hopes that the player is worth it. Every football player has waited their whole life to hear their name read at the draft. Their parents, and the fans who want their teams to have the best players and the best chance to win the season, also eagerly await this moment.

The best selection of ideas for your visibility plan is just as important as the selection of the right players for a team.

It's Draft Day!

Although you won't receive the salary of a number one pick, you do want to get the best return on your investment. That means that you need to take the time to analyze ideas that will give you the highest return on your investment of time and energy to provide the quickest shift in how you are perceived.

Nicole was very excited to go through the list that she had put together and select the ideas that she would focus on first. I shared a few additional considerations to think about as she got started. Here is the list, so you can review them as well.

- Think back to what you learned from your reflection in step one about yourself and why you want to do this. Ensure that you take those insights into consideration when you make your selections.
- Choose three to five ideas from the full list that you identified in step two of the process. You may ask, why so few? The answer is, to help you stay focused and do a great job on the ones you choose. If you try to do more, it will be harder to know if you achieve success or determine whether you need to make adjustments.
- Select the options that give you quick wins, work for your style, and are authentic to you. The intent is to have you try new actions and approaches so you can move the needle of perception, not stress you out.
- Have you considered any of the impostor syndrome traits that have impacted you and may prevent you from enjoying success? What will you include in your approach or actions to prevent self-sabotage?
- Have you chosen ideas that seem easy for you, or ones that will move you out of your comfort zone? It is my

Chapter 8

experience that clients push themselves a little, but not too far. I ask this question to get you to stop and think about what you chose. If the selections you make don't take you where you want to go, then you may need to revisit the list and choose something bigger. Keep in mind that the goal is for others to see you in a new way. This doesn't mean you have to make huge changes, but make sure they are bolder than your usual actions and behaviors.
- Set the rest of the list aside for now. You can come back to pull from this larger group as you master the initial choices you've made.

I shared with Nicole that not only would she choose ideas to pursue, it would also be necessary to think about the approach she would take, what success looks like, and determine how often to get feedback on her progress. Each of these steps will be reviewed in more detail. Bring out your notebook so you can capture your own ideas. You can build it out as a list or draw four columns, with these headings: Selected Idea, Approach, Measurement and Frequency of Measurement.

Here are the choices that Nicole decided to start with for her plan:

NICOLE'S VISIBILITY PLAN

SELECTED IDEAS:
- Schedule time with influencers to build relationships with them.
- Schedule skip-level meetings with my manager's manager and my manager's peers to build relationships with them.

It's Draft Day!

- Have more pre-meetings and post-meetings with key influencers to check in on alignment and ensure that my recommendations and ideas can go forward.
- Send status report to my manager.

Approach (How Will You Do It?)

IT IS IMPORTANT TO DESIGN your plan so that your actions help you become visible in the way that you want. Your success will come down to your consistent efforts each day, week, month, etc.

- How will you integrate these new approaches into your work life? These steps will become new habits as you do them regularly. It takes three weeks or longer to build consistency with these new behaviors. I tell my clients that this is the time to be patient and know that what they try may not work right away. Some ideas may sound great on paper, but are a different story when put into practice.
- If your action involves in-person communication—and most do—will it work best in a one-on-one meeting, in an informal conversation, or in a small or large group? Remember, you want to be strategic about what you do and how you do it.
- Be intentional in your actions. This is how they become second nature to you. What can you do to create an intentional approach that sets you up for success? Your approach to these actions is critical to achieving the results you want. A team's coach is there to guide or redirect players when necessary. Ask for help if you need advice on how to approach what you will do.

Chapter 8

- Don't overcomplicate what you say and do. This is an opportunity to share what you and your team do with others on a regular basis and in conversation. Think of it as information that can help them or provide them with insight. Share stories and successes, and talk about ways that you can add value.
- Think of your own stories and examples that you can share with people. Stories are easy for people to remember. Share the stories that include the results you accomplished and the way your leadership made a difference. The other benefit of storytelling is that it helps people connect with you on an emotional level. Think about an interview situation. The interviewer says, "I feel like this candidate would be great in that role." What makes that true for them? Whatever was shared in the interview connected well with the interviewer. Maybe the interviewee answered a question perfectly, or is from a similar background, or has an open personality that makes them approachable. The connection point could be any number of things, but the important thing is, the connection happened. People make their decisions based on emotions. Therefore, your stories are a great way for you to connect with senior leaders and show them who you are in a new way. They will remember your stories. You can do this! (Picture me with a big sign and pom-poms in my hands to cheer you on!)

Here is Nicole's visibility plan, with her approach category added:

It's Draft Day!

NICOLE'S VISIBILITY PLAN

SELECTED IDEA: Schedule time with influencers to build relationships with them.

Approach:
- Schedule biweekly or monthly one-on-one meetings with different influencers.
- Schedule lunch meetings with them when possible.

SELECTED IDEA: Schedule skip-level meetings with my manager's manager and my manager's peers to build relationships with them.

Approach:
- Schedule quarterly one-on-one meetings with my manager's manager.
- Schedule monthly manager peer meetings.

SELECTED IDEA: Have more pre-meetings and post-meetings with key influencers to check in on alignment and ensure that my recommendations and ideas can go forward.

Approach:
- Schedule one-on-one meetings when alignment is needed.
- Send out notes after meetings to capture decisions and agreements.

SELECTED IDEA: Send status report to my manager.

Approach:
- Send weekly status report to my manager via email.

Approaches to Measuring Success

WHAT WILL TELL YOU THAT the implementation of your new idea is successful? It was common to hear leaders in my company say, "What gets measured, gets managed." In other words, tracking the metrics of a project will help you create success. This "project" that is focused on you is no different. You want to be able to gauge how successful these changes are for you. Ask yourself what the specific, successful outcome is for each idea and how will you know it has been achieved. That will help you determine the best method to track your success. Refer to your answers from step one of the process to help you. Are there any ideas you would add when it comes to evaluating your progress?

You may find multiple approaches to capture what success looks like for each idea. Select ways to track the data that are simple and repeatable. You want to do this kind of metrics review on a daily or weekly basis, so it should not be complicated. Focus on simplicity to get to the core answers you need.

Below are some tips and questions you can use to evaluate your progress, suggestions for ways to gather feedback, and sample questions you can use to ask others for feedback. Choose the success metrics that make sense for your selected visibility ideas. If you add different ideas into your plan, you will want to reassess what measurements should be used at that time. Choose the tools and questions that give you the

It's Draft Day!

best indication of progress, so you can determine if and when you should move on to some new ideas.

There are various ways to consolidate the information for your evaluation step. You can use a spreadsheet, a notebook, or an app. There are many different app choices, but I find that Microsoft OneNote is an easy way to capture what happened each day and import, copy, and paste the feedback received so it is all in one place. The important thing is to keep the process simple and to be able to build it into a daily or weekly habit that you can maintain.

Self-evaluation of your progress:
- What idea(s) did you implement, and have they been effective?
- Do you feel different? Have you noticed a difference in how others behave around you? What is different?
- Do you need help from anyone else to achieve the ideas in your plan?
- What do you need to adjust or change right now?

Feedback from others:
- Ask for feedback in one-on-one meetings with your manager or other key stakeholders who will be honest with you.
- Example feedback questions to ask others (if you need suggestions):
    - I am working on (one idea or a combination of them). Have you seen me demonstrate this (new skill) in meetings or conversations?
    - Can you provide examples?

- Would you rate this skill as positive or still needs more improvement?
- Do you have any advice that would help me improve (this strategy or combination of strategies)?
- Get feedback from your designated visibility partner. What can they tell you about your progress? Do they have any suggestions for changes?
- Send out a survey for feedback from peers, stakeholders, direct reports, managers, clients, etc.
- Perform a 360-degree assessment to capture more formal and in-depth feedback from direct reports, managers, clients, peers, etc.
- Hogan, DISC, StrengthsFinder 2.0, etc. are additional assessment tools that can help you learn more about yourself and identify any gaps to work on.

Let's add in the measurement that Nicole selected for each of her ideas:

NICOLE'S VISIBILITY PLAN

SELECTED IDEA: Schedule time with influencers to build relationships with them.

Approach:
- Schedule biweekly or monthly one-on-one meetings with different influencers.
- Schedule lunch meetings with them when possible.

Measurement:
- Self-evaluation—what worked and what didn't work.

- Feedback from others—ask for feedback after meetings and send out a survey prior to performance reviews.

SELECTED IDEA: Schedule skip-level meetings with my manager's manager and my manager's peers to build relationships with them.

Approach:
- Schedule quarterly one-on-one meetings with my manager's manager.
- Schedule monthly manager peer meetings.

Measurement:
- Self-evaluation—what worked and what didn't work.
- Feedback from others—ask for feedback after meetings and send out a survey prior to performance reviews.

SELECTED IDEA: Have more pre-meetings and post-meetings with key influencers to check in on alignment and ensure that my recommendations and ideas can go forward.

Approach:
- Schedule one-on-one meetings when alignment is needed.
- Send out notes after meetings to capture decisions and agreements.

Measurement:
- Self-evaluation—what worked and what didn't work.
- Feedback from others—ask for feedback after meetings and send out a survey prior to performance reviews.

- Ask my manager for feedback in our weekly one-on-one sessions.

SELECTED IDEA: Send status report to my manager.

Approach:
- Send weekly status report to my manager via email.

Measurement:
- Verify that status report was sent each week.

Frequency of Measurement

NOW THAT YOU HAVE IDENTIFIED how you will track your success, how often do you want to ask for feedback from others? Think about this carefully as you put together your choices. Some of these ideas won't be overnight successes for you. They will take some time and require your consistent, everyday focus.

Here are my suggestions for gathering immediate and long-term feedback.

Immediate Feedback
- Ask for feedback after a meeting or at a one-on-one meeting with your manager or a stakeholder. Do this consistently so they can see that you are taking it seriously and that you want them to be honest.
- Ask your visibility partner to send you feedback after meetings. Connect with them on a regular basis so you can discuss each other's progress.

It's Draft Day!

Long-term feedback
- Schedule monthly or quarterly check-ins with your manager, peers, key stakeholders, and direct reports.
- Share the feedback that you are getting with your advisory board so they can share any ideas or insights.
- Gather feedback from your mid year and end-of-year performance reviews.
- You could also send out a survey after a few months to check on your progress. Some people will give better feedback if they can do it anonymously.

NICOLE'S VISIBILITY PLAN

SELECTED IDEA: Schedule time with influencers to build relationships with them.

Approach:
- Schedule biweekly or monthly one-on-one meetings with different influencers.
- Schedule lunch meetings with them when possible.

Measurement:
- Self-evaluation—what worked and what didn't work.
- Feedback from others—ask for feedback after meetings and send out a survey prior to performance reviews.

Frequency:
- Use an electronic app to record a daily recap of any feedback received and my self-evaluation.

SELECTED IDEA: Schedule skip-level meetings with my manager's manager and my manager's peers to build relationships with them.

Approach:
- Schedule quarterly one-on-one meetings with my manager's manager.
- Schedule monthly manager peer meetings.

Measurement:
- Self-evaluation—what worked and what didn't work.
- Feedback from others—ask for feedback after meetings and send out a survey prior to performance reviews.

Frequency:
- Use an electronic app to record a daily recap of any feedback received and my self-evaluation.
- Send out biannual feedback surveys.

SELECTED IDEA: Have more pre-meetings and post-meetings with key influencers to check in on alignment and ensure that my recommendations and ideas can go forward.

Approach:
- Schedule one-on-one meetings when alignment is needed.
- Send out notes after meetings to capture decisions and agreements.

It's Draft Day!

Measurement:
- Self-evaluation—what worked and what didn't work.
- Feedback from others—ask for feedback after meetings and send out a survey prior to performance reviews.
- Ask my manager for feedback in our weekly one-on-one sessions.

Frequency:
- Use an electronic app to record a daily recap of any feedback received and my self-evaluation.
- Capture feedback from weekly meetings with my manager.

SELECTED IDEA: Send status report to my manager.

Approach:
- Send weekly status report to my manager via email.

Measurement:
- Verify that status report is sent each week.

Frequency:
- Send on a weekly basis.

I asked Nicole, "How do you feel about your plan? Does it feel doable for you and align with your goals for visibility?"

She said, "Yes, I can see how this will change everything for me. I know it will take time for me to be seen in a different way, but I also know that I can do these actions."

I asked her, "What are your next steps to get started?"

Chapter 8

She replied, "I will send a note to each of these people to let them know that I want to cultivate a stronger relationship with them and schedule time to meet with them on a regular basis. I will work with their admin teams to get them on the calendar and plan agendas for what I want to discuss prior to the meetings."

Then I asked, "Can you see any obstacles that would get in the way of success with your plan?" She said, "No, not at this time, but I will keep an eye on my motivation and remember my why if I see that I am inconsistent. I will ask for support from you and my peers if I need it."

I shared with Nicole that as she receives new feedback, she may discover that she has some blind spots she was previously unaware of but others see in her. It is normal and happens for everyone no matter what level you are at right now.

Blind Spots

A QUARTERBACK HAS A BLIND side that he can't see when he is ready to throw the ball. If he is right-handed, the responsibility to protect him falls to the person who is the left tackle because the quarterback's blind side is on the left. If the quarterback is left-handed, that responsibility falls to the right tackle. The opposing team wants the ball, and the quarterback has it, so he needs to be protected on the field. That means these tackle positions are some of the highest-paid players on the team. Their protector role is important too. It gives the team their best chance to win the season.

In the work world, you don't have a left tackle to protect you, but you do have people who will support you and give you feedback. As you try out your new actions, it may surface that you have a few other areas to work on that you couldn't see before. These areas are known as blind spots, and they occur when the behavior or thought you have is unknown to you until someone else points it out. Some examples of blind spots could be that you don't communicate effectively, but think you do; you aren't organized, but think you are; or you are insensitive to others, but don't know it.

Nicole shared some feedback that she got from her manager on one of her blind spots. Throughout her career, she had been given praise for her detailed communication. The recognition Nicole received became her belief that her communication was good; however, as she climbed the ladder, she failed to realize that she needed to shift to a more succinct approach. She learned that she needs to speak and write more concisely to get her point across. Once she received this feedback, she focused on being more thoughtful when she wrote and presented.

Have you found or been made aware of any of your own blind spots? Do you try over and over, but still can't figure out why a certain situation doesn't get better? Like Nicole, you may have a similar example that affects your performance and becomes fuel for a negative perception of you or your work.

Be open to the fact that you probably have blind spots, and someone else may need to help you see them. That is why feedback is so important. It can help point out what you didn't know. How can you address an issue when you have no idea that it exists? I have been there, and it takes a lot of courage, vulnerability, and awareness to admit that you need to shift your behavior. With awareness that blind spots exist, you will notice and address your own.

Chapter 8

Stay Motivated

I reminded Nicole, "This is a marathon and not a sprint. Patience is important while you remain consistent and stay on the path. Remember what you responded to the questions in step 1 of the RISE process about staying motivated? Lean on those resources or find a friend to support you if you struggle with motivation, and don't be afraid to ask for help if you need it. The actions you take every day will make a difference. You may not see it yet, but it will!"

There needs to be a real shift in your behavior for people to change their perception of you. Believe me, I know that this work will push you out of your comfort zone. It will feel big to you, and maybe a bit scary (or a lot scary). Remember your goal and why you want to do this work. You want your management and key influencers to see the real you, speaking in your own authentic voice and sharing what you really think. What you do will feel big to you, but will help them see your value. Visibility is less about the size of your actions and more about their consistency and quality. The bottom line is, the actions you take to show your value cannot be done just once to see changes occur. Be consistent in what you do, and you will feel a shift in your confidence and how you are perceived.

Nicole has her plan now, and is ready to start implementing her selected ideas. How about you? Did you follow along with Nicole and build out your plan? It is time to start taking actions so that people can develop a new perception of you. Next, we will move on to the final step in the RISE process and talk about how to evaluate the success of your plan!

Actions

1. What steps will you take to identify your blind spots? Ask for feedback to help you identify them if you aren't aware of them. Once they are identified, write down what they are and how you will avoid negative impacts because of them.

2. Make a list of how you will stay motivated as you work on your plan. Whom will you call upon if you find that you've stopped progressing? If you identify a strategy now that you can leverage when needed, it will be so much easier to get back on track.

Notes

RISE STEP FOUR: EVALUATE

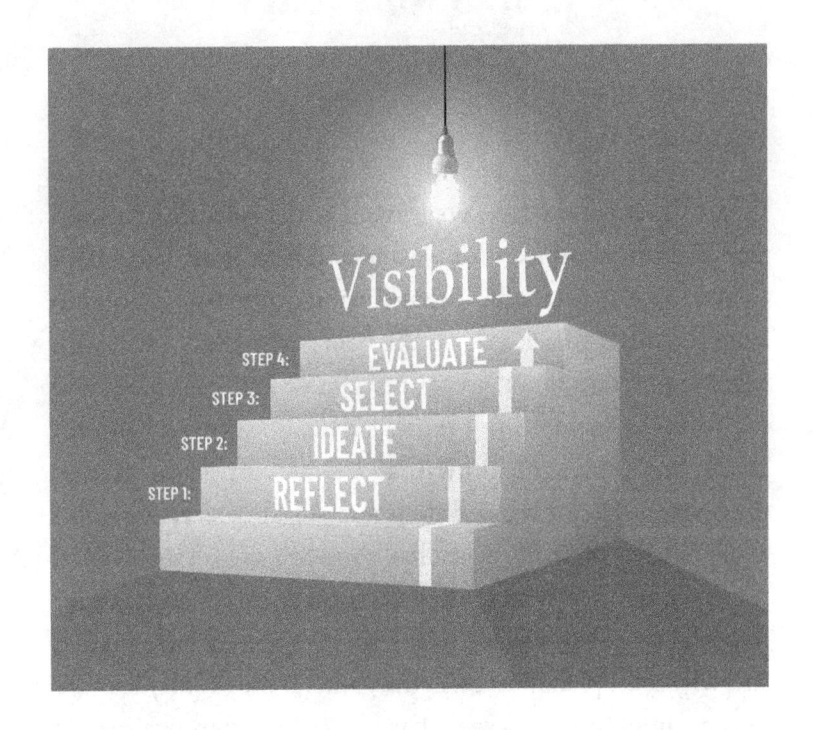

Chapter 9:
WHAT'S THE SCORE?

IN THE LAST CHAPTER, WE looked at the selection process that an NFL team uses for players and how they deal with a quarterback's blind side. The inclusion of the best players to keep the quarterback safe on the field is what helps the team win games. In football, you either win or lose; it is black and white. (Okay, sometimes there is a tie, but not very often.) The scoreboard may show that a team lost, even though they played their best and their game plan was executed as expected; the other team just had something extra that helped them score more points. After the game is over, coaches have to look below the surface to see what they may have missed and why their plan didn't win the game. If they replay footage of the game, they may see what made the difference for the other team. That helps them to adjust and prepare for the next game.

The last step in the RISE process is to evaluate the success of your plan. The evaluation of progress on your plan can be compared to the above example of a football game: It may feel as if you followed the plan, but your perception score hasn't

What's the Score?

increased yet. If it is early in the game, have patience with yourself. It takes time for people to see consistent actions and move the needle of their perception.

This evaluation process can be a little stressful, as you wait to see the feedback from your stakeholders—just like when you were in school, waiting to see what grade you got on your term paper. Be open to whatever they share with you. Whether the feedback is positive or critical, it is all information that can help you adjust your plan based on what you learn. You have plenty of time. The success of your plan must be reviewed from both an art and science perspective. You may have to look below the surface to see if you missed anything. You have the data (science), which includes specific feedback, and your self-evaluation of how you feel (art) about what you have done. It is good to look at your progress from both angles to determine how to score yourself.

A caution about feedback from others: It is easy to take on other people's feedback and give it more weight than it may deserve. If feedback comes from someone you respect, who does well with their own visibility, then you may give it more weight than feedback from someone less competent or trustworthy.

Think of feedback from peers and managers as you would the advice you get from a friend. It is only information; it isn't good or bad, it is just their opinion. You get to decide what to do with it. Does it teach you something new about yourself? Does it prompt you to make needed or wanted changes? If you disagree with the feedback, at least try to be open to it.

Chapter 9

As Nicole got the feedback from her peers, managers, and clients, she spent time analyzing what she received. She had used the feedback questions that I provided and found the process so much easier than she expected, but she had never asked for feedback before and it was a big step for her. I told her that she should be proud of herself for her willingness to be vulnerable and her courage in asking for feedback. Very few leaders take this kind of action for themselves, but it is what helps you to grow and improve.

Nicole and I talked about her plan and her progress. She had received feedback from her direct manager and some of her clients that she was ready to use as part of her evaluation. As she looked at the feedback, we walked through some questions that would help her determine the key takeaways from the data and her own evaluation.

Feedback from Others

Me: Do you see any trends in your behavior?
Nicole: "I can see that there is an opportunity for visibility from my clients' point of view as well as my manager's. They see me as smart, organized, and a great partner for them. They highlighted that I should influence others more and speak in meetings."

Me: Are you surprised by any of the information you received?
Nicole: "If I hadn't asked you for help and had these conversations, I would have been shocked. Now that we have talked about what visibility is and I understand what it means, I was more open and wasn't surprised to see their feedback."

What's the Score?

Personal Evaluation

Me: Have you been consistent and made these changes part of your everyday life?
Nicole: "I chose three options and have stuck with my plan to implement them. I think about what I need to share with people prior to attending a meeting so I can ensure that I find an opportunity to do it. If I can't share something, then I will at least work in a question to the group."

Me: Do you feel any different in meetings and conversations?
Nicole: "I feel more confident now that I have a plan to work on these actions and we have talked about how to phrase questions when I ask for feedback or statements when I say no to someone. I also use the leadership questions that you gave me." (These are in the appendix if you want to see them!)

Me: Can you see a difference in how others treat you?
Nicole: "I do feel that some people have started to see me differently. It isn't consistent at this point, though, and I think I need more time before I see a big difference."

Me: How is your motivation? Are you being patient with yourself? Do you need support from anyone?
Nicole: "My motivation is still high since I am just getting started in this process. I have some friends at work who will give me feedback, so that will help me stay motivated. After our discussions, I can see that this is not a quick fix, so I try to be patient with myself."

Chapter 9

Leadership Success Scorecard

Me: How would you evaluate yourself now on the leadership traits that you identified before we started the RISE process? Nicole responded with these self-ratings.

Leadership Trait	Rating from 1-10 (1 is low and 10 is high)
Confident	8
Strategic	7
Sets a Vision	7
Inspires Others	8
Challenges the Status Quo	7
Leads Transformational Change	7
Strong Communicator	8

Nicole: "I can see that I have made improvements with these traits since I began to focus on my plan. I try to keep these traits in mind as I have conversations and when I am in meetings to make sure that I am demonstrating them. I communicate that I am working on these specific areas when I ask for feedback from stakeholders so I get a pulse on my progress."

Plan Check-In

Me: Do you need to make any adjustments or changes to your current plan?

Nicole: "I prepare for meetings with a plan for what to say, but I also need to do that for one-on-ones and informal conversations. I missed a few opportunities to influence and share my ideas. Now that I have some specific feedback from my clients, I want to make sure that my plan addresses those areas."

Me: Have you mastered any of your ideas yet? Are you ready to shift to additional ideas?
Nicole: "No, not right now. I am still focused on the ones that I have in the plan."

Is It Working?

EARLIER, NICOLE HAD ASKED ME, "How can I tell if the changes that I make are working?" I told her that, besides analyzing her feedback, "The best way to tell if your actions are effective is by how people treat you. You will see and feel a difference in how they respond to you. Pay attention to your interactions in conversations and meetings. The changes may surprise you at first. You will ask yourself, *What happened? Did he just ask for my opinion?* You may start to feel comfortable in situations where you may not have felt you belonged before. Capture these moments in the self-evaluations each week and celebrate them! The plan is hard at work!"

I shared an example of when I could tell that things had shifted for me when I worked on my own plan:

When the executives walked into the conference room, I could tell by their facial expressions that they wondered why I was sitting at the "big table." The looks on their faces were priceless. I pretended not to notice as I smiled at them and

Chapter 9

said a big "Good morning!" *Yes! I am seated at the table with all of you. I will be here for every meeting from now on, so get used to it!*

I chose this bold way to show them a different side of me. I felt both fear and confidence as I shared an update on some of our vendors. I remember thinking, *I will tell them what I think regardless of their agreement with my decision. It is the right thing to do for the company, and they need to hear my recommendation.* It seems strange to me now—why wouldn't I tell them what I thought? However, that was one of the first times that I had used my voice, and I knew that they heard me. I couldn't believe how easy it was to do, not the big deal that I had created in my head. I sat at the table and spoke. It sounds so simple in practice, but these moves were game changers for me at the time.

Another example was with one of my team members. We had talked about a plan for her career development that would help her return to her previous function, but I knew that wouldn't happen unless we got her in front of our management more often. She was smart, but quiet and wasn't well known to them. She had to get in front of our senior management if she wanted them to approve her move.

I saw the look of fear go across her face as we talked about a presentation that she could do for them. "You want me to *do* the presentation?" I knew we would both have to do what was necessary to make her move a reality. She would need to do presentations and take on high-profile opportunities to show that she was ready for this change. She practiced her presentations, and I gave her feedback to help her prepare.

What's the Score?

I showed that I believed in her, not just in words, but also with my decision to give her a high-profile project. I spoke with the leader of the other group behind the scenes to let him know that she was interested in moving over. She initiated conversations with the right people, met with the new manager to discuss a potential role, sat at the table right along with me, and used her voice in meetings. I knew that the plan had progressed in a positive way when I started to hear people talk about her more and give her praise for her success. We had shifted the perception.

About six months later, the new group had an open position and was excited to bring her into their organization. She did well in her new role. A few years ago, she had the opportunity to move to another company and became a director, with her own team. Her success happened because of the work she did to increase her visibility and the confidence she gained. It also taught me that, as the leader in this situation, my role was pivotal. I had to support her with key influencers both in public and in private.

It was important to share these examples with Nicole so she could see that visibility is a journey. I told her, "I didn't know how to do it and neither did my team members. What I learned changed everything for me. I learned how to take these actions and to teach others. I had worked on this for quite a while and the results showed. It had a ripple effect on my team and people I mentored. Once I got the gist of how this worked, it was as if a switch turned on in my brain and it became focused on ways for me and my team to gain visibility. The skills that had been so hard for me became second nature."

Chapter 9

Post-process Evaluation

I CONGRATULATED NICOLE FOR THE work she had done on the RISE process so far! Although we would continue to work on her visibility, she had learned how to do it on her own. I encouraged her to keep her focus when it seemed as if progress was slow.

Maintain the consistency that you have started to cultivate. You have experienced behavior changes and increased awareness, and made shifts in how you see yourself. Not everyone will see these changes yet, but have compassion for yourself and don't give up! This simple process will help you build your confidence before you know it. When you feel good about what you do, your confidence grows and everyone can see and feel it.

I encouraged Nicole to stay motivated and in a positive place. I wanted her to be resilient enough to deal with setbacks. I give you the same advice. Your thoughts and beliefs can still sabotage your progress. This isn't to bring you down in any way, but to remind you to keep your eyes wide open and aware that pitfalls can happen. It is easy to run into challenges and fall back into old patterns when you try something new. Self-doubt can creep in and impact your progress. I know that I have said this before, but: Stay on the path. You are about to turn a corner and step into a more visible version of yourself. You can do this!

When Nicole and I met again six months later, she bubbled over with excitement. I could see that she had some great news to share. I urged her to tell me. "Don't leave me in suspense, what happened?"

She began to share. "You remember my manager told me that I needed to become more visible? He gave me my performance review last week and told me he couldn't believe the change in me! He received great feedback on me from his peers as well. The RISE process worked! I can't believe it!"

This was not the same Nicole that I had first met, a woman with slumped shoulders, tears in her eyes, and no hope for her career. Now she was full of confidence and excited about her career possibilities. The work that she had done had paid off. The conversations she'd had with the management team and influencers had changed the game for her.

She continued, "I haven't told you the best part yet!" She took a deep breath and said, "They asked me to lead a new, high-profile global program that will give me a new team and huge exposure within the company. They said they were excited to see me lead this effort! ME!!! Can you believe it?"

I was so happy for Nicole. She had done the work, and it made all the difference! Now that she knew how to show others her value, taking on this new role would be the first step of many to come in her successful career.

I have seen too many situations where people disengage and feel stuck, with no way out. That was how Nicole used to feel. However, that experience was in the past now. All the hard work she had done was worth it, and she was ready to celebrate like she had won the Super Bowl!

I hope you see that you can do for yourself just what Nicole did. I can't wait to pop the virtual champagne for you and all your success!

Actions

1. Finish your plan, if you haven't had the chance to yet.

Chapter 9

2. Share your successes with me! Send an email to hello@susanmbarber.com and let me know how your visibility plan is working for you! Put "My Visibility Plan Is Working!" in the subject line and share the details! I will send you a personal note of congratulations! I can't wait to see what you accomplish with your visibility!

Notes

Chapter 10:
IT'S TIME TO STEP UP!

WHEN MY IT TEAM AND I designed a new system, we had to build it to handle all possible scenarios for that specific business process. For any of my techie friends, you will know that we create a use case for each of the scenarios. A use case explains the business process of the scenario and then shows the way that the system will respond to each of the process steps. To use an ice cream metaphor, we categorized these scenarios. We would start with the "vanilla" version. This scenario was the most basic and would handle most of the transactions in the new design. Next, we would look at the "rocky road" versions. These were the more complicated scenarios that didn't happen as often but still needed to be addressed.

Up until now, we have talked about the vanilla versions of how to apply visibility. Are you ready for an unexpected situation when it happens? This chapter is about the unusual ways that leaders need to be visible in rocky road circumstances. The normal rules don't apply, and leaders have to find ways to become—or stay—visible through some tough, stressful experiences. As you read these examples, think about how you would take your visibility to the next level under these conditions.

Working Remotely

AS I WRITE THIS CHAPTER, one of the biggest rocky road moments ever has happened. It's 2020, and you know what that means—we are in a global pandemic. It is a scary time for everyone. To try and stop the spread of COVID-19, everyone except essential workers has to quarantine at home. Many people who have never worked from home are now forced to do so and help their kids with e-learning on top of it. The overall uncertainty and devastating impacts of the virus have challenged everyone's stress and anxiety levels. Leaders have had to take mental health concerns into their conversations with employees and find new ways to stay engaged with their teams.

This pandemic has pushed the boundaries for the workplace and challenged long-held beliefs that work must be done in an office. We will see new changes come into play as we evolve in a post-pandemic world. Some people will return to an office or split their time between work and home and others will continue to remain at home full-time.

Leaders and their teams have been forced to get creative to achieve results, and it has pushed them out of their comfort zone. They must think about how to get their work done in a new way. The option to walk over to someone's desk for a conversation or the ability to pull a file out of a cabinet are no longer available to us, at least for right now.

Chapter 10

The first few months of the pandemic triggered fear and anxiety as we moved from a short-term quarantine to an extended remote work situation with no known end date. Once the initial fears passed, we moved into a "new normal." People began to think about what the long-term implications of a remote work environment might be for them. You can perform your job in a remote environment, but how do you make sure people know what you do when they can't see you? How do you know what your team does when they aren't at their desk nearby?

The positive outcome here is that this forced remote work situation has opened people's eyes to what is possible and, in many ways, it has leveled the playing field; everyone has had to adjust. Remember when you used to stop by someone's office, or you'd have a conversation as you got a cup of coffee down the hall? That wasn't possible for many over the last year-plus.

This is a moment when you have to think out of the box to create intentional conversations. Remote work may be more of the norm in the future, and actions to show your management what you do will have to be done differently. Your actions will need to be especially intentional and focused to ensure that you are in front of your leadership as often as possible. We talked about some examples for getting in front of your management in step two of the RISE process, but they may need to be modified when you are not in an office. Technology has helped with remote work to some extent, but interactions aren't the same as they are in person and it can make you feel disconnected.

One of my clients, Kris, has been able to work in a remote location for a few years. Although the remote work option was her choice to be closer to her extended family, she wonders if it might limit her chances for advancement. We coached through various situations she has faced and some ways she can remain top-of-mind with her management.

Perhaps addressing some of the challenges and concerns about remote work could be helpful to you if you are new to it or lead a team that works from other, separate locations. All these situations can have an impact on how you are perceived and your ability to stay connected with what happens in your organization. I will share the questions that I asked Kris. She gave me permission to share her responses.

1. **Challenge #1: It can be difficult to stay updated with information when I'm not there in person.**

   Me: "What could you do to stay updated with information?"

   Kris : "I could have additional one-on-ones with people who are in the know and could provide me with more updates. I could also be more engaged in the meetings I attend and ask additional questions. This approach would help me be more visible and ensure that I know more about what's happening."

2. **Challenge #2: It can be harder to observe direct reports and give them feedback.**

   Me: "Are there other ways that you can get feedback on your team?"

Kris: "Since I can't be in the office to observe them, I could ask a few of my peers who are in the office (or others who are in more meetings with them) to provide feedback on them. I also want my direct reports to expand their own networks so they have additional people to leverage when they need help if I am not available. I have a few people in mind who could answer questions if needed, and it would help them build a stronger relationship with my team members."

3. **Challenge #3: I miss out on hallway conversations to get informal information.**

   Me: "What could you do to get informal information instead?"

   Kris: "This one is hard because those conversations happen so often, and people don't think about it. I guess the best thing I can do is schedule time to connect with the people I would normally have had hallway conversations with in the past to hear the latest updates. I could meet with some additional people as well. That would be a positive outcome of this situation because I may not have done that before."

4. **Challenge #4: Peers may be able to advance faster because they are in the office and get more time with management.**

It's Time to Step Up!

Me: "What could you do to get more time with management and be visible to them?"

Kris: "I knew that this was a risk for me when I chose to go remote full-time. I have other colleagues who are remote, too, so I am not the only one who struggles on this one. If I think about how to do this in a different way and stand out, I will need to be more intentional. I travel to the office quarterly, but if they let me, I think every other month would be better. I will schedule key face-to-face meetings and perhaps lunch or dinner to get in as much face time as possible. The other thing I could do is to send regular status reports and other resources to my manager and clients, so they hear from me more often."

5. **Challenge #5: I'm unable to attend social gatherings, like lunch or happy hours after work, so I have far fewer opportunities to network.**

Me: "Are there options to network in a different way?

Kris: "Hmm. I hadn't considered another way. I meet with the same people all the time in one-on-ones. I should expand my circle to meet with others in the organization and ask for ideas about who else to meet with outside of my group. I also want to attend more conferences and meet with affinity groups that are now offered remotely. I can take advantage of those opportunities as well."

6. **Challenge #6: It is hard to be impactful when you attend meetings virtually.**

   Me: "What could you do to be more impactful in virtual meetings?"

   Kris: "Sometimes it is hard to hear, and I hate having to ask people to repeat a question. I guess I could request that the leader repeat questions for everyone on the phone or on video so that we can all hear it. I know others struggle with this, too. I could take notes so I am forced to pay attention. I can also prepare for meetings so that I have my ideas ready for the discussions. I need to find opportunities to interject my thoughts and ideas, and that is no different than it would be in person. I can't let my remote work situation be a limiting factor."

7. **Challenge #7: It is difficult to observe political dynamics when you aren't in the room or the office.**

   Me: "What could you do to learn about the political dynamics?"

   Kris: "I need to be intentional when I am in the office and watch for those dynamics. I could also rely on some of my peers I meet with to share their observations. I guess until now, I have assumed that I must see people to understand the dynamics, but it is also important to listen to what they say. If I focus on that, I may learn just as much as I do when I watch over videoconference or when I am there in the room."

8. **Challenge #8: I may miss out on opportunities because management wants people to lead programs or projects in person.**

    Me: "Is it true that you can't lead when you aren't there in person?"

    Kris: "No, I guess that isn't true. I could let my manager know that I am interested in additional opportunities to lead. I could also volunteer to support the person who oversees the work so that they can be successful. I need to have a conversation with my manager about my career. We talked about it when I decided to do this, but it makes sense to have another conversation to see what opportunities exist for me to lead from here. Some of these thoughts that I can't lead outside an office are my own limiting beliefs. I have operated under the assumption that it isn't possible for me to lead from here, but people lead global teams remotely right now. I need to eliminate that story and ask for what I want."

Remote work is now more of the norm versus the exception. Intention, focus, and consistency will ensure that you stay top-of-mind with your management as they consider you for new opportunities.

Chapter 10

Ready or Not?

I picked up the phone with a big smile on my face as I imagined the congratulatory conversation that my client and I were about to have.

I was wrong.

It was around 5:00 p.m. on a Monday night, the first time I could breathe in what felt like forever, and I sat at my desk. When the phone rang, it startled me and interrupted the first moment of silence I'd savored in months. I looked down and saw my biggest client's name on my phone display. My team and I had successfully implemented a big project over the weekend for this client that was the culmination of eight months of work.

My client said, "The order-processing system has a major problem. I can't be sure if it is because of the changes that your project made, so that is why I wanted to call you first. It was the only major change that went in over the last twenty-four hours." *Oh, no, this can't be happening...* He continued, "Sue, I know this isn't good news, but this issue has ground the system to a halt. No one can trust any of the information that they see on orders." I wanted to cry, but there was no time for that.

He continued, "The statuses on every order in the company are different than they were twenty-four hours ago. We can only ship what was picked prior to the change." I knew what this meant from my experience when I worked in our distribution center. We had a window of about twelve to twenty-four hours to figure out what was wrong. Any timeframe longer than that would cause major delays in shipping to our customers, and all the production facilities and distribution centers would be

It's Time to Step Up!

at a standstill. I couldn't yet begin to process everything else that would be affected.

My heart just sank. All the work we had done would be perceived as a failure if we had screwed up the system.

The client asked if I could get my team to look at the system. Most of the team had already gone home. We had celebrated our success earlier that day, and now I might have to tell them we celebrated too soon. I felt so bad after all the hours we had just worked, but there was no other choice. I called everyone on my team and shared the news that we had a huge problem to solve.

We worked until 4:00 a.m. and still didn't reach a full understanding of what had caused the problem. I drove forty-five minutes home to sleep for an hour and take a shower before I headed back to the office for a 7:00 a.m. status update meeting. Everyone from the entire systems and business management teams was there. They could tell I hadn't slept much by how bloodshot my eyes were. *Why didn't I grab some Visine?* It had been a long night for me and the team. I am not sure how I gave a coherent update, but I did.

At the end of that day, we found out that another person in another group had made a change that they thought would have no effect on the system. It wasn't our project after all! I said a silent prayer of thanks.

At that point, I wondered if I should turn the issue over to someone else, since it had nothing to do with our team; but after I'd spent twenty-four hours straight on it, that didn't make sense. My team helped to fix all the orders to get them back the way they looked before the issue started. I saw it through until it was resolved.

Chapter 10

These moments are not for everyone, but I thrive on them. I can feel the adrenaline kick in and my sense of calm does, too. One of my gifts is the ability to take over a situation that most people would turn and run from, rally a team when they are exhausted, and still get a good resolution. It is how my brain works and, with a problem such as this one, it is a gift. I had been able to work on systems issues for years, and that credibility is what got me into IT in the first place. This was a high-exposure leadership moment, without a doubt. It showed my management that I continued to own an issue and would see it through to completion.

When this crisis occurred, I was a novice in terms of this type of situation and was thrust into the spotlight in less than twenty-four hours. It was rough, but it could have been so much worse, and it was a chance for me to show people what I could do. I had a good reputation, but my management needed to see me operate at a higher level. I didn't know it at the time, but that crazy issue was a pivotal moment for my career. I got a two-level promotion not long afterward because of how I handled everything.

You can't predict when these opportunities will come along, so it is important to always be ready to take advantage of them. Be prepared to show what you can do. Let your management see a different side of you and the capabilities you possess.

One thing is for certain when you work in a company: Change is a constant. Business needs change, employees and managers come and go. The ability to deal with ambiguity and adapt to change is necessary. Situations will occur that are out of our control and, as leaders, we need to be ready, even when we aren't. Some people may call that trial by fire, and it happened throughout my career. It taught me how to think on my feet and deal with whatever came my way.

I was great at execution and could solve issues, but I didn't talk about what I did; I just did what was needed and moved on to the next thing. Do you do that, too? A strong work ethic is great, but people have to see you, and you have to talk about what you do well.

Major Changes (Acquisitions, Divestitures, Layoffs, etc.)

MAJOR CHANGE IN ORGANIZATIONS PRODUCES high levels of anxiety and stress. Whenever there is an acquisition, divestiture, layoff, or business downturn, it brings uncertainty for employees who want to understand what the change will mean for them. The search for answers becomes the primary goal. If communication is limited, employees look to their leaders to try and figure out what the answers are and how the team will be impacted. Leaders are put in the tough position of needing to be visible both to their team and to the organization and to answer questions as best they can and defer the rest. Transparent communication is necessary, wherever possible, to enable stability and help teams through the change process. This is the time when leaders have to face their teams while they process the changes themselves.

Remember in Chapter 1 when I talked about how the amygdala in your brain can't tell the difference between a real or a perceived threat? It causes your fight, flight, or freeze reaction to kick in and your stress level to increase. If you work in a high-stress, high-change environment, there will always be some issue to deal with and your brain will feel as if it is in danger all the time.

Leaders feel that high stress in these situations more than others because they are the representatives of management to their teams during big organizational shifts, but may not have all the information yet or be able to share their opinions. They have to be cautious about what is shared, smart about how they position information, strong under pressure, and calm under stress that can challenge the best of leaders. It is more difficult when they don't know how the change will impact them, either. They have to carry on and be mindful of their reactions and what they say because everyone watches the leaders in these moments.

Although your instincts would tell you to avoid conversations because you don't know what to say, in these situations you have no choice but to be more visible than ever. The teams that work for you and the rest of the organization need your support, so you can't hide. This is a whole new level of leadership. You can't show the emotions and anxiety that you feel. You have to wear the brave face and take action every day.

What is the best way to lead while on this rollercoaster of change, stress and anxiety? I have been through acquisitions, divestitures, workforce reductions, and spin-offs throughout my career, and it doesn't get easier. Each announcement of a change of this magnitude makes your stomach turn upside down and your mind go in a million different directions.

I know you may think, *Hey, Sue, haven't you suggested that leaders should be more transparent?* Yes, I am a huge advocate for that, but it isn't always possible in this kind of situation. You must keep your team calm, and you can only communicate what you can share. This is not the normal, everyday situation. I'll share what I did to maintain as much transparency as I could during a major transition.

Our CEO announced in March, 2015, that our company had been purchased by 3G Capital and would be combined with the Heinz company. This news brought so many unknowns, possible impacts, and questions to my mind that would need to be figured out. Our company had always been in the dominant role as the acquirer. This time we were no longer able to call the shots. I knew that my team would be struggling with this news and what the change could mean for all of us. I had to quickly build trust with my team about the circumstance we had in front of us. My goal was to provide as much clarity as I could and maintain my composure to keep everyone else calm, too. I was honest and said that I may have information that I couldn't share, but that I would disclose what I could when I was able to share more information. They needed to know that I would be straight with them and they would hear information from me first. I think we all knew we had to face that, at some point, some people would have to leave the organization.

If you are in a similar situation, it is important that you have an outlet. Leverage your peers and management for support. This is important for two reasons. First, you need to be able to talk about what's happening. You also need to use the opportunity to gather information from each other. This informal information channel helps you put the puzzle pieces together and figure out what is on the horizon. This is where you show your value. The communication from your management is the "official" channel of information, but may be inconsistent. You need to engage in "unofficial," informal communication to see the big picture. It helps you figure out the current circumstances and what is next so you can be prepared. This is when you have to plan for how you will answer some of the toughest questions you will ever get. You can't hide. You have to be there for people. It isn't the same kind of visibility I've talked about so far, but it is one of the most important ways you can support a team.

Be transparent with your team and let them know that this change is a struggle for you, too. Share what you do to manage your own stress if it will help them. This does not detract from your leadership, but shows that you are able to be vulnerable. Employees will connect with you and be more open to talking about their own experiences. Not all leaders will do this, but I found that when I did, it brought the team closer together throughout a difficult time.

Major organizational changes are beyond stressful for everyone, but especially for the frontline leaders. I remember that each morning, I sat in my bedroom in the dark and breathed slowly to try and stop the pain I felt in my chest before I went into the office to face another difficult day (it wasn't a heart attack; it was stress and anxiety). I had to be strong for my team, but it took a toll on me.

I remember that, when we first heard the news, we all experienced some grief and wished that the announcement wasn't true. It is normal to want that, but when you continue to hope for it, you delay the acceptance of what is, which prevents you from seeing the new opportunities that will arise because of the change. I learned how to look at the positives that the change would bring for each of us. I knew that we had all been through a lot as an organization, but we would be okay. That certainty allowed that stress I felt to go away. Once I accepted the situation, it was easier both to manage for myself and to help others get through it.

Time for a New Role

SOONER OR LATER, YOU WILL move into a new role either at your current company or a new one. When Nicole moved into her new role, we built out the next version of her action plan. Each time you change roles, it is a best practice to revisit the RISE process and see what you need to do to take your visibility to the next level. The expectations of a leader grow as they move into their next role, so additional actions may be necessary to demonstrate new leadership traits in a bigger way. Go through the leadership success scorecard and determine the traits that are needed for this type of role so you can exceed expectations as you create your new plan.

I interviewed two of my former colleagues about their transitions to new companies. I was curious about how they viewed the level of visibility needed to succeed in a new company. Both took lateral positions in new companies and new industries, excelled, and then moved into VP roles. I want to share some of their great advice about what helped them succeed in their new companies.

Janet recommended the below suggestions that helped her get two promotions, to senior director and VP:

- Advice from one of her mentors: "You have a choice; do you want to be a leader who maintains stuff or a leader who creates the future?"

Chapter 10

- Get on projects with high-exposure opportunities and look for ways to show results.
- Look for roles that provide opportunities for transformation.
- Raise your hand and take on a new challenge. Help others see you in a different light.
- Communicate in a proactive way and make it meaningful. Focus on outcomes.
- Continue to find ways to establish your worth so you are always viewed as valuable.
- If there are people in a meeting whom you haven't met, introduce yourself and schedule time to meet with them.
- Be comfortable with being uncomfortable.
- Step back and figure out what type of leader you want to be; don't just operate on autopilot.
- Mentor junior team members to help them build their skill muscles for the next level and give them opportunities to get in front of influencers.
- VPs must make bigger decisions, communicate more, and amplify messages across a larger part of the organization.

David shared these experiences and nuggets of advice from his transition and advancement to VP:

- One of his mentors told him never to lose an opportunity to share what you do with people. That mentor introduced him to influential people and made it clear that it was David's responsibility to maintain the new relationships.

- As a result of a company separation, many of David's supporters in management went to the other company. He had to build his network all over again. His advice is to always keep your network strong; it is "money in the bank" that you can use when you need it.
- David created wins for himself as he learned about his new company's business and talked about it in one-on-ones. He created a one-pager that included accomplishment highlights and personal information and sent this to people ahead of meetings so he could build relationships with them.
- The time he had to network was focused and intentional. He volunteered to do activities outside of his area of responsibility so more people would know him.
- He found roles that intersected with other functions so he could build relationships and create value.
- Although he was more of an introvert, David learned that it was his responsibility to manage how he was perceived and stay in front of the right people.
- He believes that women and those in underrepresented groups have to do more to make themselves stand out. His recommendation is for them to work hard, but also be willing to tell people what they do so they get noticed.
- Categorize people so you spend your time in the right places. Sponsors should receive more of your time than mentors. Ensure that you provide more information about what you do to the people who can help you the most.
- Create the perception that matches who you want to be as a leader.

Chapter 10

These ideas can be used for any role change, but both Janet and David proved that you can be successful in new organizations. They had to be intentional as they worked through their transitions so they could not only succeed, but advance.

Actions

1. Make a list of the ways you will be visible to your management if you work remotely.

2. What would you do as a leader during a major transition? Write down how you will lead in a visible way under stressful or challenging circumstances.

Notes

Chapter 11:
IT'S YOUR TURN TO SHINE!

DID I HEAR HER RIGHT? I thought to myself. Does she really think her voice doesn't matter?

I stood at the island in our kitchen and put away the leftovers from dinner as my daughter shared about a date she had planned with her boyfriend. He had told her what he wanted to do on their date, but he wasn't interested in what she wanted to do. She told me, "I don't really want to do what he wants, but I guess we can just go, because what I want to do doesn't matter." I steadied myself as I walked over to the kitchen table and sat down. I asked her to share more about it. She added, "Sometimes it is just easier to do what he wants to do rather than fight about it." What she said triggered memories in me, and I had a flashback from thirty years earlier in my own relationship.

I was taken back to who I was in high school and college. I gravitated toward the friends and boyfriends who had the confidence that I lacked. If they wanted to go somewhere and I wasn't that excited about it, I just kept that to myself and said nothing. If there was an argument, I would shut down and give in instead of attempting to fight the battle. I would keep it all inside until I couldn't anymore. What I held onto was all this negative energy, and the other person had no idea I was upset. It wasn't fair to them not to share what I felt at the time. All these experiences came back to me in a rush as I listened to my daughter. I was grown now, but inside I was still that same young girl who kept everything in. I hadn't changed at all.

My focus had been on becoming more visible in my professional life. Until this moment with my daughter, I had no idea that I had not been vocal or visible in my *personal* life. She modeled my behavior and followed my lead. I would have been happy for her to be similar to me in any other situation, but this was not good for her. The beliefs she had taken on were mine and they would not serve her in the future. She would continue to give others the power and the stage that she should have. I needed to set a better example, and it had to start right now.

Later that night as I got into bed, I shared the conversation that my daughter and I had had with my husband. I leaned my head back on the pillow after I told him what happened and said, "She learned how to be this way from me. I have buried what I didn't want to deal with my whole life. I can't let her wait until she is in her forties to figure this out for herself. I need to show her that it is okay to speak her opinion and not keep quiet. She wants harmony and is afraid to disagree with someone because she thinks it will harm the relationship." I sat up in bed, but paused before I made my next statement: "I have to be the one to set an example for her. The wife you married is gone as of right now. You will see someone new, who speaks her mind and no longer keeps quiet to avoid conflict."

Chapter 11

It was a bit dark in the room, but I am sure he showed a bit of surprise and wondered exactly what that meant. It was time to let go of the part of me that settled, didn't use my voice, and spent too much time worried about everyone else. That person wasn't who I wanted to be at work or at home, either. I had not made the connection before that this was something that needed to be addressed in both parts of my life.

I had adopted this habit of staying quiet and avoiding conflict when I was young, and it continued into adulthood. It allowed me to maintain harmony with others and keep that crown of perfection on my head that you read about in Chapter 1. My husband said, "You shouldn't keep quiet when you are upset, and we should talk about it. I don't want our daughter, or any of our kids, to not be able to speak for themselves." I know that I shocked him a bit, but he needed to know what this change meant. He had to understand where this change in me came from and that I believed it would help me, our kids, and our marriage. What I did from that moment on would be the opposite of what I had done for so many years. I wouldn't hold myself back from what I wanted to say anymore. I wouldn't drop out of a discussion because it was easier to avoid conflict and minimize arguments. I wouldn't settle for what I didn't want. I felt empowered in that moment in a completely new and different way. I stood up for myself and knew that it was what I needed to do so my kids would see that they could do it, too.

I had tried to be superwoman every day and that wasn't good for me, so I delegated more of what needed to be done around the house to everyone else. It wasn't that they wouldn't have done some of this stuff before, but that I had chosen to do it all.

I took other small but visible new actions. For example, when it came to discussing options for where to eat, I didn't automatically go along with everyone else's choice. If I disagreed with my husband, I said what I thought, and we discussed family issues in front of the kids. I used to try to keep these discussions from them to protect them, I guess. I thought they would worry if they saw their parents disagree in front of them, but it was good for them to see that you can have difficult conversations and work through them as a couple. I had to learn how to eliminate criticism and judgment from what I said and focus on an assumption of positive intent on the part of the other person in every conversation. I also started to accept what occurred in my day with a more neutral mindset to limit the ups and downs and stay in a more positive place. My actions haven't always been perfect, but over time the increased awareness and focus on who I wanted to be shifted my behavior and set a better example for my kids.

Lessons Learned

As I learned new lessons, I put them into practice myself and then taught them to my team and my family. It made it easier for me to quickly adapt them from one context to the other. We had different topics to discuss at work than at home, of course, but my goal was the same: Help them learn how to use their voice, stand on their own, and gain confidence.

For example, at work, situations would come up in one-on-ones with team members. Once they explained a scenario they were struggling with, I would ask them questions—in the same way I do now as a coach—to see if they would handle it differently the next time. I would share stories and talk about my own experiences so they could see that they weren't the only ones who had been through it, and share what I did to resolve each situation and how I learned from it. Our discussions would completely shift their energy. They would release the tension they held in their shoulders and they would sit back in their chairs, much more relaxed, for the rest of the conversation as we talked about ways to handle the situation and that it was okay to ask for help.

At home, I wasn't sure that my actions to be more visible would have the intended impact on my family, but they have in ways I couldn't have expected. The whole family shifted because of the changes that I made. I know it may seem out of the ordinary to share more about my family with you, but I want you to see the ripple effect that occurs when you change; everyone around you, whether at work or at home, will change, too. For example, although it is easy for my daughters to have a disagreement over text, I ask them to have a real conversation, in person, so they can hear each other's position and work through whatever the challenge is. This has helped them learn how to have difficult conversations both with each other and in other situations at work or with friends.

I am proud to say that my daughter has gone from deferring to a boyfriend and letting him make all the choices to being someone who stands on her own today. She told me, "I am a catch, Mom. If they don't want to be a part of my life, that is fine with me. I don't need them."

I am so proud of how far my daughter has come. I've watched her confidence in herself and her self-esteem grow. She took the role of assistant director at a daycare and leads her own staff of teachers in the middle of the pandemic. As the only leader on-site at times, she has had to step up to have difficult conversations and maintain calm in the midst of chaos when they are shorthanded. She has a heart of gold, advocates for every child in the daycare, and is now a leader on her own leadership journey.

My other daughter is a resident assistant at her college dorm. She is a born leader and has leveraged what she's learned to rise to the occasion in multiple situations. She has had to facilitate tough conversations with people on her floor who have had issues with a roommate or struggled with mental health challenges during COVID. And she has had the courage to stand up for what she believes in and advocate for the students to ensure that they received the help they needed. Although she was initially anxious about going away to school, she has grown so much and was recognized with multiple awards for her college leadership this year. She has pushed herself out of her comfort zone to become a visible leader not only in her dorm, but also as a director in the student government and on campus with multiple organizations.

My son is the best example of someone who stays neutral and only rarely strays from that state. When he does get frustrated about something, as teenagers do, he shares what has happened and knows I will listen. He is so smart, and he has taught me about creativity and patience and not to make assumptions. He is learning how to use his voice in a bigger way and I can see how his sense of humor will serve him well to diffuse tense situations. Humor is a great way to help everyone open up more and talk through whatever has happened.

If I compare life at home with how things used to be, it isn't perfect, but there is so much more laughter and joy in the house. My husband and I also have better conversations with each other and with the kids. I used to be critical and want everything to be perfect for them. I didn't know that my need for perfection was projected onto them. The lessons I learned increased my confidence, my value, and my self-worth. I can see the positive effects that these lessons have had on all of us. This journey has been a catalyst of change for me, and has had a ripple effect on everyone around me.

I think about the moment in the kitchen often. What would have happened if I hadn't changed my actions? I have faith that my daughter would have learned these lessons, but possibly much later in life. No one should ever settle and take less than they deserve, which is what can happen when you let people or things into your life that don't serve you. Don't allow the diminishment of who you could be!

What Have You Learned?

I promised you at the start of the book that I would help you understand what visibility is, why you need it, and how to take actions to raise your visibility with your management. My hope is that I have been able to model what I have learned for you. I shared my stories so you could see that you aren't alone, and I shared the most impactful stories that caused me to shift my behavior and my perspective. I have made mistakes and done my best to learn from them.

Here is a quick recap of what you have learned throughout this book:

- Hard work is important, but it is not enough to show others your value.
- Visibility gives you a platform to show what you can do and helps decision makers picture you in a higher role.
- You can shift a negative perception into a positive one.
- One of your best tools for doing this is following a well thought-out action plan that uses the RISE framework to include the approaches that fit your authentic style and can be adjusted to create the outcome you want.
- You can increase your visibility through the use of small steps that are intentional and consistent, and that create a shift in how you are seen by your leadership.
- The potential obstacles that could get in your way include: your thoughts, self-sabotage, impostor syndrome, and external events that are out of your control. You can leverage the suggested strategies to deal with these challenges.
- It is possible to create visibility under difficult circumstances, and those circumstances can create new opportunities for you to show your capabilities.
- Greater visibility can have a big impact on your career and your confidence.
- Trust yourself and focus on what you want. You don't need to compare yourself to others or be someone else anymore. You can be yourself and become the leader you were meant to be.

It has been many years since I began this journey, but it seems like it was yesterday. Originally, I made the choice to be invisible in my career and only wanted to focus on hard work.

I had to learn some tough lessons and ask for help from others to move past my fears and choose this more visible path.

Decide each day how you can intentionally use your visibility. What if your intention is not only to stand for your own success, but also to stand for the success of those around you? You can take what you have learned and support them with opportunities to learn and grow. The value and confidence inside of you will be unleashed, to your benefit and others', now, because you made the choice to read this book, create a plan, and act!

Nicole's Lessons

REMEMBER HOW EXCITED NICOLE WAS when she heard the feedback from the management team and got her new role? Is that the type of story you would like to share about yourself someday soon? I want that story for you and to be able to cheer you on.

I asked Nicole, who went through the RISE process in this book, what she learned and what advice she would give to someone who is about to try it. Here is her feedback:

"I thought the process itself was easy to follow. I was reluctant at first to rate myself on the Leadership Success Scorecard and answer the questions in step one, reflect, although I knew that I should. It made me feel vulnerable, but then I was so surprised at what came out of the exercise! I replied to the questions that you had in the reflection step and that helped me learn about myself and where I held myself back.

"Going through the second step, ideate, was very helpful. The ideas on your list were simple and included choices that I had not considered before. This step made me think about what my strengths are and what ideas I could implement that were more my style. It also helped me think of some new ones that would make sense for me to try, and I was excited to get started.

"The third step, select, was much broader than I thought it would be. I thought it was only focused on how to select ideas, but then I realized it was about approaches to take and how to capture the data for tracking success. It was good for me to define everything before I implemented any of the ideas. I have always struggled to ask for feedback. This step helped me to decide who I should ask for feedback, and then you gave me the questions that I could use. That made it so much easier! I have always struggled to know what to say to management, so that was good to have.

"The evaluate step is where I spent a lot of time after I started to try out the ideas. I went through my own feedback as well as the comments from stakeholders. It was an insightful process because they identified some blind spots that I couldn't see. They knew that I wanted their honesty, and they delivered. They gave me feedback that was constructive, but also gave me positive feedback that I would never have heard without this process. I was so grateful to learn how to apply this feedback to my plan and adjust. I set time on my calendar to go through my plan each week. I reviewed what I learned, what worked and didn't work, and what I would do next. The process was simple to follow and made it easy for me to implement the changes. It was impactful to see my scores increase when I went through the Leadership Success Scorecard again and could rate myself higher. That didn't seem feasible before I started this plan.

"My advice to anyone who wants to increase their visibility is that this is the easiest process I can imagine to help you get there. You have to do the work, be intentional and consistent, and also have fun!

"Capture the feedback on your progress each day so you can review it each week. It is so much easier to have that ready rather than try to remember it all. I could see how much I had grown when I looked at the first few weeks of my notes.

"Be consistent in meetings and conversations. If your leaders only see you use these new approaches occasionally, they won't believe that any real change is in process. Follow your plan and think about what you want to share each week. What do they need to hear from you, and what is important for you to share?

"The last thing is to have fun. This type of change is important to your career, but that doesn't mean that you can't have fun with it! I saw that people responded to me in a different way once I started the new actions, and that reinforced what I did.

"I know that I shared a lot, but this process has truly changed me and I am excited to continue to grow! I couldn't see that it was possible to shift this much at the start, and now I am proof that it can happen if you want it!"

Create Your Authentic Visibility

IF YOU ARE STILL IN the midst of your plan, I thought you might like to hear some additional feedback from others who are on a similar path. One of the participants recently contacted me to let me know that he applied what he had learned in the class and had accepted a promotion. I was thrilled for him! Here is the feedback from a few of the Create Your Authentic Visibility course participants after they completed the RISE process:

- "Before taking this course, visibility was already on a list of priorities that I had identified for myself. But I was unsure of where to begin, so this course came at a perfect time for me as I begin to explore growth opportunities in my career. Throughout this course, I was able to do a lot of self-reflection that helped me identify what was holding me back from putting myself out there and being visible. It was refreshing to hear from peers that they were also feeling some of the same feelings I had, though all our paths and long-term goals were different. Now I am more self-aware and can take small steps toward 'showing up for myself' and my team! The RISE process made it easy to map out a clear plan and set expectations and goals for myself along the way. I am excited to share these ideas and processes with my team, as they too want to gain more visibility!"
- "I understood what visibility was before the course but struggled with how to achieve it. After the first session, I was able to see what I wanted to achieve with a visibility plan, and why. I also learned that it wasn't difficult to create visibility. Small steps, done consistently, can make a huge difference! I would recommend this course to anyone who wants to move ahead in their career or wants to be noticed more for achievements and abilities in the workplace."
- "This class really opened my eyes! Visibility is such a powerful tool to use in so many ways. Since taking this

class, I have been more confident in my current role at work, and it has given me a new outlook! I recommend that everyone take this class and learn ways in which they can be visible—it can lead to so many great opportunities."

RISE and Shine!

WHEN I WAS YOUNG AND it was time for me to get up for school in the morning, my dad would come in and say, "Rise and shine!" Of course, that wasn't what I wanted to hear… I wanted more sleep! Now, every time I hear the acronym RISE, I can't help but finish the sentence Dad used to say each morning… "and shine!" Little did my dad know that I would write a book about visibility. He had no idea that it would include a process called RISE and have lightbulbs on the front cover as a metaphor for shining on leaders. Divine intervention, maybe? Thanks, Dad!

I didn't know it when I started to write this book, but I still wore some of my old, invisible armor and wasn't ready to let go of it yet. It has been a journey over the last four years for me to get comfortable enough to share the stories in the book with you. Although it wasn't easy to drop the armor, when I finally did, it allowed me to be vulnerable enough to share the stories, resources, and examples that would help you the most. I hope this book has inspired you to be authentic and to be vulnerable enough to let down your armor if you still wear it.

You did it! This is the final step in your journey. Visibility is now a choice for you to take advantage of and leverage as a leader. There are so many benefits for you. It helps you shine a light on your value, builds your confidence, and creates opportunities for you to take your career to new levels and help others do the same.

What is Next for Your Visibility?

NOW IT IS YOUR TURN! Think about who you were when you picked up this book. You may have been someone who struggled with your visibility, but not anymore! You have the tools, strategies, and resources you need to show your value to others. You now have everything you need to create your visibility whenever you want it.

Can you see that the visibility you have created is bigger than just a possible promotion? What does it give you that you didn't have before? Visibility creates new possibilities, like influence, opportunities, and a platform to elevate others and drive real change. What do you want to create with your visibility? If you think about it, like Nicole, you now have an opportunity to leverage and scale your leadership in a bigger way for yourself and for others. You have so many gifts that the world needs to see and that won't transpire if you don't share them. Do you have a dream inside of you, but haven't dared to think about it yet? Remember, this isn't only about your career, it is also about your life and how you want it to be!

This book was written to help you create the visibility that you need to help others see your value, but more importantly, it is for you to see your own value, maybe for the first time. The value is in the real you, confident and able to stand alone without need for a suit of armor or a mask to hide behind. You have everything you need to break through your fears, stand

Chapter 11

in your own power, and become the authentic visible leader you were meant to be. Go make it happen!

Actions

HERE ARE SOME WAYS TO tap into my support and that of my community! Come join us!

- Join my Be Bold, Be Visible, Be the Leader You Were Meant To Be Facebook group[43] to connect with other readers of this book!
- Check out my videos on the RISE Process and other free resources on my website: https://susanmbarber.com
- Would you share on social media that you just finished the book and tag it with the #thevisibilityfactor in your message? Be sure and tag me so I can cheer you on and continue to bring you encouragement!
- If you feel called to leave a book review on Amazon, that would be great! It will help get this book in front of other leaders who haven't yet heard how important visibility can be for their careers. You can also share the book with leaders who would benefit the most. Thank you!
- Share your successes with me! Send an email to hello@susanmbarber.com and let me know how your visibility plan is working for you! Put "My Visibility Plan Is Working!" in the subject line and share the details! I will send you a personal note of congratulations! I can't wait to see what you accomplish with your visibility!

Appendix

Resources

Be Bold, Be Visible, Be the Leader You Were Meant to Be Facebook group: https://susanmbarber.com/fb-group/

Go to my website for videos on the RISE framework, RISE process examples, additional resources, and blogs on leadership and career transition topics: https://susanmbarber.com/

"Visibility for Leaders" infographic (ideas for visibility): http://susanmbarber.com/wp-content/uploads/2017/03/Visibility-for-Leaders.pdf

Questions for Leaders

MY FAVORITE LIST OF QUESTIONS that can be leveraged in meetings to help you use your voice. These questions can be modified as necessary for your industry, culture, etc.

- What does success look like? How will it be measured?
- What are the risks? Is there a mitigation plan in place to deal with them?
- What are the issues?
- What alternatives were considered?
- How does this compare to what is in the industry?
- What do our competitors do in this space?

- What is the communication plan?
- What is your approach for implementation?
- What is your action plan to get back on track?
- How is the team morale?
- What does your experience tell you?
- What concerns do you have?
- What are the outstanding decisions that need to be made?
- What is the best recommendation, given these challenges?
- Have you gathered input from the clients?
- What is the feedback from the rest of the team?
- How does this align with our goals or strategy?
- What is the business case for this work, and how will it be funded?
- Have you aligned with your clients on this change?
- What value can you add to build a relationship?
- Can you assume positive intent in someone else?
- What is your responsibility in this situation?
- Can you say more about that?
- Can you play back what you will do on this request so I can ensure that we are aligned? (This allows both parties to ask and answer questions about what the outcome should look like.)

RISE Framework Step One – Reflect: Additional Examples

Nicole's answers in Chapter 5 were an example of someone who is a senior manager who wants to get a promotion. The below examples are for a director and VP level in the first step of the RISE process.

Director Level – Will

Will leads a global team for his company. They have been focused on a companywide project for the past two years and have run into multiple issues. Will feels a lot of pressure from his management to implement on the planned go-live date. He believes that they will figure out the issues, but he isn't sure if they will make the date. His management had confidence in his ability when they gave him the project, but he feels as if they have lost confidence in him. He needs to turn things around fast or risk the loss of his credibility.

The Why Questions:

Me: Why do you want visibility?
Will: "I need to create a level of confidence with my management. I had the confidence before, but it has recently shifted with a project that hasn't gone well. I need to find a way

to communicate more effectively and influence conversations in a better way."

Me: Why is it important for you at this time in your career?
Will: "The positive perception others had of me is in jeopardy and needs to be salvaged. I will need to be visible to them and communicate what is realistic for the team to accomplish."

Me: Why do you think others feel that you need visibility?
Will: "My VP said that I should already have come to my senior leadership team to discuss the issues of the project with them. I wanted to show them that we could handle it and figure out the issues. I didn't want to get all the questions that would come out of that conversation, so I had hoped to avoid it."

The What Questions:

Me: What will visibility bring to you?
Will: "I will show the leadership team that in tough situations, I can stand up and be accountable. My team needs to see me as an example and that I support them. I have not done a good job with my communication and influence with the leadership team. I need to be able to demonstrate confidence if I have to deliver hard feedback."

Me: What holds you back from visibility?
Will: "I think it is my fear of failure. I don't want to embarrass myself in front of my leadership team. I know that they put a lot of faith in me to deliver this and I want to avoid a tough conversation."

RISE Framework Step One – Reflect: Additional Examples

Me: What do you want other people to see that you can do?
Will: "I want them to see that I can lead through this challenge and implement the project. It is more important that I face them instead of hiding—that isn't who I want to be."

Me: What if you don't make any changes and do what you have always done?
Will: "I am not sure I want to think about what will happen if I don't turn this around. I could get demoted or lose my job."

The How Questions:

Me: How will you evaluate your success with your visibility plan?
Will: "If I start to get good feedback from my manager that he sees a difference in me. I will attend the staff meeting to present updates and share what our plan will be to turn around the project. If management is supportive of my leadership and my plan, then I will feel as if the visibility plan is working."

Me: How will you stay motivated if something you try doesn't work well?
Will: "I know that I can be my own worst critic. I will talk to you about it as my coach and check in with peers I trust to keep me motivated."

Me: How will you gather feedback from others?
Will: "I will ask my manager for feedback in my one-on-ones. I will also ask my senior leadership team for input in my one-on-one meetings with them."

Me: How do others promote themselves?
Will: "I can see that other people do this in an effective way. They share in meetings and sell the story about the positives and the negatives for their projects. I thought I was too, but that was when things were good. I can see that when things were more of a challenge, I held myself back. I haven't failed before and this feels as if I am."

Me: How can you apply what others do to your own visibility strategy?
Will: "I will put myself on the senior leadership agenda every two weeks to provide updates. I will also have conversations with some of my peers and mentors to see how they handled these kinds of situations before."

The Who Questions:

Me: Who are the important stakeholders who need to see your visibility?
Will: "My manager, my leadership team, my peers, and my clients."

Me: Who can give you feedback on your progress and results?
Will: "My manager, but also my clients, direct reports, and senior leadership."

Me: "With whom could you work out a visibility partnership?" (This is where you help to promote what a partner works on and they do the same for you.)

RISE Framework Step One – Reflect: Additional Examples

Will: "I have done this for my peers, who are great at these things. I can't ask them to support me yet, but once I start to take new actions, I will ask for their help and support."

VP Level – Michelle

MICHELLE JOINED A GLOBAL COMPANY as a VP of finance a few months ago. She had not looked for a new role, but they recruited her to join the company. She had been a VP at her previous company, but it was a smaller organization. She knew that the role she took on involved a much broader set of responsibilities than she had held before. She was excited and nervous to go through her onboarding process and hit the ground running.

The Why Questions:

Me: Why do you want visibility?
Michelle: "I was hired by the company a month ago, and I need to get connected to the people on my team, my clients, and my management team."

Me: Why is it important for you at this time in your career?
Michelle: "My success in the first ninety days of this role will be dependent on my success in creating positive visibility with the people in the organization. I need to build trust, establish my credibility, and build relationships to accomplish the goals we have in this group."

Me: Why do you think others feel that you need visibility?

Michelle: "My new management team has high expectations for my success at the company and will look for me to hit some key milestones quickly. If I don't build the relationships and respect, I won't have the chance to motivate the team to hit our goals. I am sure they also want to prove that they made the right choice for this role and the visibility that I create is one way to validate that."

The What Questions:

Me: What will visibility bring to you?
Michelle: "Visibility will help people see who I am, since they don't know me at the company yet. If I can show them that I am open and listen to them, it will help them see that I care. I also want them to see what is important to me and how I can help them be successful, and that will go a long way toward a successful transition."

Me: What holds you back from visibility?
Michelle: "I don't think there is anything major that holds me back, but I want to do a good job in this transition. It overwhelms me to think about remembering all this new information and how many people there are to connect with. I will have to pace myself and take a lot of notes so I can put it all together in my head."

Me: What do you want other people to see that you can do?
Michelle: "That I can lead a big team and drive change across the company. I knew that I signed up for a big agenda of cost reductions across the company. I will have to deal with

RISE Framework Step One – Reflect: Additional Examples

pushback, and I need to get those relationships in place so we can align on the goals that need to be met."

Me: What if you don't make any changes and do what you have always done?
Michelle: "When you join a new company, it means you need to demonstrate what you can do within a short time. I don't have the luxury of the brand equity to carry me that I had at my former company. I need to deliver a plan and lay the groundwork for change in the first three months."

The How Questions:

Me: How will you evaluate your success with your visibility plan?
Michelle: "I will ask for feedback from people, but I think that at this initial stage, it will be important to see how they respond to me in conversations. How much do they share with me, and are they engaged when we meet? This will be my initial measurement."

Me: How will you stay motivated if something you try doesn't work well?
Michelle: "I know that I will need to be patient and recognize that there will be days when things don't go well. I will keep focused on the big picture and trust that I can do this job well."

Me: How will you gather feedback from others?
Michelle: "I will focus on my manager, peers, and clients at first. They are the people that I will work with most. I will ask

them for feedback on my transition and if there is anything else I should focus on."

Me: How do others promote themselves?
Michelle: "I don't know enough about how people do it at this company yet. I have seen my share of people who create visibility well and those who only want to brag. It is something that I will watch as I begin to get more involved."

Me: How can you apply what others do to your visibility?
Michelle: "I will have to revisit this one after I have established myself and understand more about the culture at the company."

The Who Questions:

Me: Who are the important stakeholders who need to see your visibility?
Michelle: "My manager, my leadership team, my peers, and my clients."

Me: Who can give you feedback on your progress and results?
Michelle: "My manager, direct reports, and other stakeholders that I can ask to give me feedback, too."

Me: With whom could you work out a visibility partnership? (This is where you help to promote what a partner works on and they do the same for you.)
Michelle: "I will have to revisit this one as I get to know people I can establish this type of relationship with at the company."

Endnotes

Introduction

[1] Suzy Frisch, "3 Scientific Links Between Handwriting Your Notes and Memory," Redbooth.com, August 3, 2016, https://redbooth.com/blog/handwriting-and-memory

Chapter 1

[2] Brené Brown, *The Gifts of Imperfection* (Center City, MN: Hazelden Publishing, 2010)

[3] Merriam-Webster.com, definition of "visibility," https://www.merriam-webster.com/dictionary/visibility (last accessed July 26, 2021)

[4] James Allen, *As a Man Thinketh* (originally published 1903), The James Allen Free Library, http://james-allen.in1woord.nl/?text=as-a-man-thinketh

[5] Allen, *As a Man Thinketh*

[6] Maya Angelou quote, Goodreads.com, https://www.goodreads.com/quotes/7273813-do-the-best-you-can-until-you-know-better-then (last accessed July 26, 2021)

[7] Marian N. Ruderman and Patricia J. Ohlott, "The Realities of Management Promotion," Center for Creative Leadership, 1994, https://www.ccl.org/wp-content/uploads/2015/04/RealitiesMgtPromotion.pdf

[8] Harvey Coleman, *Empowering Yourself, The Organizational Game Revealed* (Bloomington, IN: AuthorHouse, revised edition, 2010)

[9] Be Bold, Be Visible, Be the Leader You Were Meant to Be Facebook group: Facebook.com, https://susanmbarber.com/fb-group/ (last accessed July 26, 2021)

Chapter 2

[10] Shelley J. Correll and Lori Nishiura Mackenzie, "To Succeed in Tech Women Need More Visibility," *Harvard Business Review*, September 13, 2016, https://hbr.org/2016/09/to-succeed-in-tech-women-need-more-visibility

[11] Correll and Mackenzie, "To Succeed in Tech Women Need More Visibility"

Chapter 3

[12] Byron Katie and Stephen Mitchell, *Loving What Is: Four Questions That Can Change Your Life* (New York: Harmony Books, 2003)

[13] Byron Katie website: https://thework.com/ (last accessed July 26, 2021)

[14] Byron Katie website: https://thework.com/ (last accessed July 26, 2021)

[15] Be Bold, Be Visible, Be the Leader You Were Meant to Be Facebook group: Facebook.com, https://susanmbarber.com/fb-group/

[16] Herminia Ibarra, Nancy M. Carter, and Christine Silva, "Why Men Still Get More Promotions Than Women," *Harvard Business Review*, September 2010, https://hbr.org/2010/09/why-men-still-get-more-promotions-than-women

Chapter 4

[17] Brad Yates website: https://tapwithbrad.mykajabi.com/ (last accessed July 26, 2021)

Endnotes

[18] KPMG International, "KPMG Women's Leadership Study: Moving Women Forward into Leadership Roles," KPMG.com, 2015, https://home.kpmg/content/dam/kpmg/ph/pdf/ThoughtLeadershipPublications/KPMGWomensLeadershipStudy.pdf

[19] Tara Law, "Women Are Now the Majority of the U.S. Workforce — But Working Women Still Face Serious Challenges," Time, January 16, 2020, https://time.com/5766787/women-workforce/

[20] Katie and Mitchell, *Loving What Is*

[21] Byron Katie website: https://thework.com/

[22] Matthew Biddle, "Men Are Still More Likely Than Women to be Perceived as Leaders, Study Finds," University at Buffalo School of Management, August 6, 2018, http://www.buffalo.edu/news/news-releases.host.html/content/shared/mgt/news/men-still-more-likely-than-women-perceived-leaders-study-finds.detail.html

[23] Biddle, "Men Are Still More Likely Than Women to be Perceived as Leaders"

[24] Be Bold, Be Visible, Be the Leader You Were Meant to Be Facebook group: Facebook.com, https://susanmbarber.com/fb-group/

Chapter 7

[25] Carl Richards, "Learning to Deal with the Impostor Syndrome," *The New York Times*, October 26, 2015, https://www.nytimes.com/2015/10/26/your-money/learning-to-deal-with-the-impostor-syndrome.html

[26] Steven Pressfield, *The War of Art: Winning the Inner Creative Battle* (New York: Warner Books, 2002)

[27] Vanessa Van Edwards, "Impostor Syndrome: 5 Ways to Overcome It and Thrive," Science of People, https://www.scienceofpeople.com/impostor-syndrome/ (last accessed July 26, 2021)

[28] Pauline R. Clance and Suzanne A. Imes, "The imposter phenomenon in high achieving women: Dynamics and therapeutic intervention," *Psychotherapy: Theory, Research & Practice*, Volume 15, #3, Fall, 1978

[29] Terry Gross, "Tom Hanks Says Self Doubt is 'a High Wire Act That We All Walk,'" *Fresh Air Podcast*, National Public Radio, April, 26, 2016, https://www.npr.org/2016/04/26/475573489/tom-hanks-says-self-doubt-is-a-high-wire-act-that-we-all-walk

[30] Rachel Sams, "Are You an Impostor? Phenomenon makes executives doubt their own abilities, skills," *Baltimore Business Journal*, June 20, 2008, https://www.changingcourse.com/pressrelease/baltimorebusinessjournal06202008.htm

[31] Van Edwards, "Impostor Syndrome"

[32] Paulo Coehlo, "On the Importance of No," PauloCoehloblog.com, June 9, 2012, https://paulocoelhoblog.com/2012/06/09/on-the-importance-of-no-2/

[33] Brené Brown, "3 Ways to Set Boundaries," *O, The Oprah Magazine*, September 2013, https://www.oprah.com/spirit/how-to-set-boundaries-brene-browns-advice

[34] Lao Tzu, *Tao Te Ching*, trans. James Harris (Independent publisher, 2020)

[35] Olin Miller, comment page 4, column 2, *Reno Evening Gazette*, December 19, 1936, https://www.goodreads.com/author/quotes/6420834.Olin_Miller

[36] Tanya Geisler, "The Praise You Seek and The Criticism You Avoid, Two Sides of the Same Coin?" TanyaGeisler.com, https://tanyageisler.com/blog/seek-praise-avoid-criticism?rq=criticized

Endnotes

[37] Elizabeth Gilbert, *Big Magic: Creative Living Beyond Fear* (New York: Riverhead Books, 2015)

[38] Brené Brown, "Why Brené Brown Says Perfectionism Is a 20-Ton Shield," *Oprah's Life Class*, Season 3, Ep. 315, October 6, 2013, https://www.oprah.com/oprahs-lifeclass/why-brene-brown-says-perfectionism-is-a-20-ton-shield-video#ixzz6zckA3thj

[39] Brown, "Why Brené Brown Says Perfectionism Is a 20-Ton Shield"

[40] Brown, *The Gifts of Imperfection*

[41] Brown, *The Gifts of Imperfection*

[42] Jess Winans, "Retiring Perfectionism," *Times Union*, January 11, 2018, https://blog.timesunion.com/jess/retiring-perfectionism/281/ (last accessed July 26, 2021)

Chapter 11

[43] Be Bold, Be Visible, Be the Leader You Were Meant to Be Facebook group: Facebook.com, https://susanmbarber.com/fb-group/

Acknowledgments

To my husband Mike, and to Manda, Kelly, and Jackson: Thank you for all your support as I took on this crazy dream of writing a book and starting my own business! You have never doubted for one second that I could do it, even when I had my own doubts. You are my world and I love you all so much!

To my sister Debbi: You are one of the strongest people I know, and you inspire me every day. This is the time to use your voice and choose what makes you happy.

To the rest of my family and friends, who motivate me, make me laugh, and are always there when I need you: You are all a blessing in my life.

To all the great team members who worked for me or with me: I learned so much from you. Each of you taught me how to be a better leader and I am so grateful.

Thank you to Karen Davis, Suzanne Coonan and all the coaches in my life who had the courage to give me honest feedback so that I could become a better leader and coach. Some of those lessons were harder to learn than others, but I am grateful to have learned them from all of you.

To my former managers and mentors: Thank you for all the guidance and opportunities to grow and develop that you gave me on my leadership journey. You have made a difference in my life. I have learned so much from all of you and appreciate all the advice, coaching, and mentoring along the way.

To my clients: Thank you for trusting me to be your coach. It has been my honor to see you grow and develop into amazing leaders. This book wouldn't be the same without your stories, suggestions, and ideas.

A special thank you to AJ Harper, Laura Stone, the WOW Sprint Group, and the Top Three Book Workshop Group: This book would not exist without all of you. This was a dream that has now become a reality, and it is so much better for all of your support throughout the past four years. I am so happy to be a part of this community, and eternally grateful to all of you!

About the Author

SUSAN M. BARBER, FORMER FORTUNE 500 Director turned Executive Coach, helps business leaders who want to play bigger, increase their visibility, and, finally, shine a light on their leadership strengths so they can elevate their position in the workplace. She brings strong business knowledge to her coaching from 25+ years of experience at Kraft Heinz where she successfully held multiple leadership roles before leaving to marry her love of people development and her passion of helping companies solve business challenges. In her book, *The Visibility Factor*, she shares stories, actionable advice, and an easy-to-follow process for readers to create authentic visibility for themselves. Susan lives in the northern suburbs of Chicago with her husband and their three children.

What are my stories / limiting beliefs?

   I don't like the spotlight, attention —
     it was bad as a child to be the
       center of attn —
         Stay hidden — it was safe — physical
         && emotional.
     HOLD BALLS super — you don't get hurt.
     Saying your piece, your opinion — w/ others
       don't agree isn't worth the pain,
       the heartache, the disappointment
      want to be easy, liked, loved

   Being distant is safe, keep you away from
   hurting me,
   disappointment.

   Don't make plans, they can change, people will
   be disappointed. Can't count on others —
   they disappoint me.

   I'm not a risk taker, I follow the Rules
   I'm not a party person, extrovert. I like calm
   quiet, I don't brag, talk over others —
     humble, kind. →

Personal critic says, that I'm not perfect,
I don't know what I'm doing in this job, as a
new manager, of exec search, I am small,
others don't need to know or want to know —
   It's not important to take up space.

Send prior deck to
every hiring leader?
our wh. deck?

bio each team members impact

- Set an intention each day
  to find ways to take action

> My mission...
> to ensure that people
> knew that my group
> added value and supported
> our clients well.

☆ Every interaction is a chance to
let that person know what you do,
or my team does. AND stay top
of mind for any new opportunities

Amy — USP — Share digest of comms course

her key takeaways

that you will do as a result of the class?
& why?
Acceptable

Development plan next 3 months.

- You need to share what you know
- you were hired for a reason
- mgmt doesn't know what you do + your team

Tell them what you think — they may not agree with you but need your insights to make good decisions.

Say what you think no matter what you fear.

Ideas

- Mauricio - visibility cover?
- Share w/ TALT - Global search results trends - stat total
  w/ Meddie + JT - Alumni pilot
- Capability - Dorothy? Amy, Caroline. Curry?
- Qtrly connect - Amy take lead from Jen to get AWon Track / Amy Orly
- Asger quarterly time search
- Shona - respond search from rule.
- Sarah from TM or shared inplace?
- ISC scouting PM updates
- HRBPs/VPHR - about what?
- Networking events - ARGs.
- Local San Diego chapter
- ESX + Thrive
- Agencies

take the lead to share what you + your team have done

- Skip level w/ Asger for visibility